# The Juggle Is Real

by Molly Grantham

This book is an original production of Miss Meade Publishing
Charlotte, NC
Copyright ©2020 by Molly Grantham

Cover design by Diana Wade
Text design by Diana Wade
Cover photography by Emby Taylor
All rights reserved

I have tried to recreate events, locales, and conversations from my memories of them. I have only used the first initial of a person's last name when quoting their post from a public Facebook page.

ISBN: 978-0-9994302-5-5

*To Necessita, the goddess of destiny.*
*There is no goddess of surprise, but there should be.*
*None of us know what's next.*

# INTRODUCTION

My first book felt like a fluke. As if divine intervention had aligned the stars to bring an idea to life—an idea that would actually sell in stores, with lines at book signings. I never breathed through it. Never stopped to take in the moment and think, *I am a real author.*

I didn't feel like a real author. That's not compliment-fishing or lack of confidence, just the truth. I played down the Herculean efforts it took to get published. Kept rolling on as if writing a book was no big deal. Just another thing. Tack it on to my days. Don't brag, don't self-promote too much. I put *author* in my bag of party tricks and let it sit there, usually just gathering dust.

Writers are like that: always worried they're not good enough. They spend hours, days, and years pulling out their hair, pounding tables and sobbing through a keyboard, as they dig and dig to find the exact right words to string together emotions and thoughts they see clearly in their own heads. They spend thousands of dollars and eternities trying to get their words published or picked up by an agent. They dream about characters at night, wake up with vivid descriptions, and scribble hazy ideas in a notebook beside their bed before they float away. Then, after spinning and draining their souls, climbing and clawing to craft their thoughts into something someone could read, they shoo away flattery about their work when it's finally published, and even—this is so shameful—self-deprecate and put themselves down.

It makes no sense. But I've learned there is a common thread between fiction and nonfiction authors: fear. Writers won't willingly jump into conversation about what they've written out of an insecurity over what a judge and jury (you the reader) might think.

Yet here I am, jumping in. Again. Another book.

Why go through all that a second time? Because as scary as it is to put yourself out there with your thoughts and words—especially when you write tough truths about your family and the personal journey of learning to love your own children—my need to write is so intense that at times I feel like an addict desperate for a hit. I'll be short-tempered and shaking until I find a keyboard and pull up an empty Word document. I pull over when driving to rummage through the console for a working pen so I can write on the back of a receipt, or napkin, or my daughter's summer camp application. I catch myself sending overly descriptive texts to good friends. They sometimes reply, sometimes not; either way it doesn't matter. It's not about their response. It's about me getting thoughts out and sending them to someone. I write when I'm bored. About anything. About my personal hates and huge loves. In an airport, I pass strangers and make up stories about these people I don't know. I think about how I could describe the hat they have on, or their inappropriate travel shoes, or the specific look a mother wears when she's dragging luggage and two children.

Words have weight. Words hold power. I love words so much that I sometimes read another author's words, and if they zing with personality and truth, I underline the sentence and take a picture of it on my phone to go back and review their brilliance whenever I want.

I write because it makes me feel full. Happy. Not because it's always seen by others or even good—there is nothing more unattainable as a writer than the perfect sentence—but because simply getting the thoughts out makes this addict content.

My first book, *Small Victories*, was an unexpected project. As a journalist, I storytell about other people as a fly on their walls, so writing closely about my own reality was an uncomfortable, peculiar feeling. The book originally started as Facebook posts during maternity leave when I was trapped inside my house with small children and missed working . . . missed adult interaction and the moving world outside. I was—and am—beyond lucky to have a daughter, a son, and a career, and though one of those things remains not like the other two, I knew all were pieces of me. I just couldn't find anyone else saying it was okay to love your job AND your kids. Confessing those feelings in a sometimes-funny, sometimes-raw way helped me in those critical first weeks and months.

*Small Victories* started on Day Six of my second child's life and went up through Month Thirty. When I go back to read whatever page haphazardly opens, I smile at the various memories that unspool. But after a few paragraphs of reading, I think of better words I could've used, and put the book down out of self-imposed humiliation.

You know, being a writer.

As a glass-half-full woman, however, there is a hands-down best part about both *Small Victories* and this new book *The Juggle is Real*: the stories are truth. Someday, Parker and Hutch will hold their childhoods in their own hands. I also love that the visceral portrait of their lives ends up reminding many of you about your own children, your own grandchildren, your own desires, your own life as CEO of your household with no paycheck, or your own life as a working parent. Through your Facebook comments, your lives have ended up in front of my face, and I included some of your thoughts in both books because of the beautiful insights many of you have passed on. We all live different situations, but we find similarities. I thank you deeply for sharing.

*Small Victories* ended with three words: *To be continued* . . . Turns out they were the three most personally challenging words in the entire 323 pages. I wrote them before having a way of knowing how the book would be received, and by publishing them, I subconsciously built in a guarantee to myself that I wouldn't cop out on writing a second.

This second book starts much differently than the first. *The Juggle is Real* picks up where *Small Victories* left off in its afterword . . . inside a hospice house with my mom. In that sterile room, I was editing a memoir about how I became a mother while watching mine die. It felt very full circle.

You're about to read Month Thirty-One. It begins right there. Right after her death, seen through my eyes, observing my children.

A writer is a writer. Always. Someday, maybe, I'll write a gorgeous novel with characters created from my never-sleeps mind, but right now I've got stories happening to me, around me, inside me, and in front of my face. Not an afternoon or night goes by when I don't see or experience something I could write about. Sometimes laughable. Sometimes upsetting. Sometimes joyful. Often magically ludicrous.

I once again hope you enjoy the journey . . .

. . . I still enjoy living it.

—Molly

*I want to do something splendid . . .*
*Something heroic or wonderful*
*that won't be forgotten after I'm dead . . .*
*I think I shall write books.*
—Louisa May Alcott

# MAY

## MONTH THIRTY-ONE: My Kids and My Mom

How much of *now* do children remember later?

I have recently beaten my brain digging for this answer.

It has been a long few weeks.

Despite her chemo-defiance and objections, we had to put my mom in hospice care at the end of April. Home visits began two days after this picture was taken. You maybe can't tell—she still looks beautiful—but metastatic breast cancer had taken over her liver, and from this moment until May 19, it was an aggressive decline. One Parker and Hutch could have had a front row seat to watch if I'd let them.

I didn't let them. I didn't want them to remember their Grammy as thin and sick. If at the ages of six and two-and-a-half they later recall anything about her (*will they?*), I wanted the memory to be vibrant, fun-loving, goofy and full-spirited.

A gift for them, but also a gift for her.

If things had been different this past month, I might be writing about how Hutch is graduating from a crib to a big-boy bed. How he doesn't sleep and comes to get either me or my husband, Wes, every other hour, every single night, for the past four weeks.

But that thought pales in comparison to this other one that popped up as Mom's skin sallowed and changed. To sit here and write about trying to make a child stay put at 2 a.m. would seem insignificant.

C3&0

Death is a difficult thing to navigate with young children. Some people want to give their children a chance to say goodbye at the bitter end. Others, no way. As long as the choice on how to handle it is made with love, it's probably a good one.

I didn't need Parker and Hutch to have a final moment with Grammy, but I did go back and forth a hundred times on managing other specifics. At what point should I stop taking them with me to sit on her back deck and look at the lake? They loved watching the boats, but at what point should I protect them from her stumbling speech and cloudier mind and visible physical changes?

Wes said it was up to me. My mom, my choice.

In trying to decide, I kept returning to:

*What will they remember?*

Childhood memories are elusive. Inconsequential moments can be vivid visions; other bigger moments you wish you could recall are empty. My first memory from growing up is from the age of three . . . older than Hutch now, younger than Parker. My parents were showing me how to open the drawers in my new dresser. They got divorced months after that day that I can close my eyes and still see. It's a fleeting recollection, and the next memory doesn't come until my fifth birthday party, when I was running on a front lawn. Then more from age six, and around seven and eight there's an avalanche of mental snapshots.

One really powerful childhood thought I have is from seventh grade: I'd gone to visit my strong and hearty grandfather, suddenly in the hospital with pancreatic cancer. He looked very different, very small, lying in a hospital bed. That one moment is mixed in with years of amazing memories of him from before, yet it's one of the first images in my mind when someone says his name.

I wish my twelve-year-old self hadn't seen him that way.

Because of those personal reflections, I landed at a place where soon after this photo was taken, Parker only saw Grammy one other time. It was on that back deck overlooking the boats they both loved. We opened birthday cards people had sent my mom, as she was two weeks from turning seventy. Time wasn't on her side. We knew it'd be smart to open them early. Parker helped us read them aloud in her kindergarten voice. For me, that was enough. She's an astute six-year-old. She would surely be impacted by, and possibly remember, an immobile Grammy. Or maybe worse, an unable-to-speak Grammy. I didn't want to put those thoughts in her beautiful little head and chance a fun memory being replaced with a sad one.

I don't deny what happened to my Mom—cancer is very real. One in three people live with it, survive it, or die because of it. Metastatic breast cancer, Mom's second go-round with this disease, is a twist on the typical diagnosis. Doctors tell you, "It's livable, but not curable."

That's true. Metastatic *can* be livable. But isn't always. No more evidence needed than the past three weeks of watching my mother turn from my mother into someone I didn't recognize.

Crazy enough, I turned forty the week we took her to the hospice house. Talk about a peculiar, self-reflecting birthday. It was not a marker of moments and held no celebration. Instead, I spent that morning and afternoon holding my mom's hand in her hospice bed, talking with gentle words and fake jokes. I asked if she knew her baby girl was having a birthday, and if she herself remembered turning forty. I recalled childhood memories of us playing double solitaire, endless swim-team practices, and the catering business she'd run decades before out of our home. I laughed about our epic teenage girl/mother fights. The ones you think you'll never get past, but always do. I rubbed my thumb over her blue veins that suddenly seemed more visible on her sun-spotted hand, and listened to deafening silence in response. She was in a coma. I sat there staring at those arched, unmoving cheekbones and told her how beautiful she was. How lucky I was that now at forty, I could look forward to having her ability to age with grace.

I never got anything in return from her that day. No squeezing of her hand in response, or eyes fluttering as sometimes patients do in the movies. I just kept talking, wondering about a birthday spent watching your own mom die.

Eventually, my loving and dedicated brother, Jay, came in to relieve me. He'd driven up from Atlanta to take a twenty-four-hour shift. I had to drive straight from the hospice house to work. WBTV News had been more than accommodating these crazy three weeks, and I was only showing up for two hours that day—cruising in at 9:30 p.m. just to do the 11 p.m. news—but I had to go. I had 4-inch heels and a dress in my car to change into at the TV station.

My entire life could depend on telling you what news stories were relayed that night or what I said and reported and acted like I understood, and I'd never be able to respond. I was a machine, going through motions with no feeling. At the end of the newscast, my co-anchor at the time surprised me. He and the producer had found funny photos to broadcast, with our 11 p.m. team singing a rendition of "Happy Birthday." I laughed and played it right . . . I think. I can barely remember that special moment they were trying to create. My emotional receptors were numb.

When I got home after midnight, there were two massive pink helium balloons the kids had left floating near the kitchen counter. One big 4 and one big 0. Parker had written a card, Hutch had drawn scribbles, and Wes had left them out with a cupcake.

It was at that moment, and only that one, seeing their crayon cards and childlike "I love you!" that I cried.

Life can be tough. Everybody has their own struggles. But when I think about it, my main one these past few weeks hasn't been cancer or hospice or even dealing with my mother's death; it has been trying to figure out how to maneuver through all those things with kids. I just wasn't sure I wanted them—especially Parker at her age—to have visible toughness be what they might remember.

But will she remember the sunshine on the back deck? Or reading Grammy's birthday cards? If she even remembers Grammy at all? And even though I'm okay with that one light-filled day being Parker's last visit, did I shortchange my daughter? Here comes devil's advocate . . . did I take away Parker's opportunity for closure? Will she later resent me because I didn't trust her enough to handle a final conversation with a grandmother she adores?

Time will tell. So far, though, Parker seems comfortable with how it played out and the basic explanation that Grammy was sick and went to join other good people in Heaven.

By comparison, we did take two-and-a-half-year-old Hutch to see my mom at the hospice house. He went only once and wasn't there long. I don't think he'll recall anything about the sterile room or the quiet grandmother, but I felt good about the decision to have him more involved that day. He brought joy to everyone sitting around her bed.

These past few weeks have been a great reminder that there's no rule book: we simply do the best we can. My mom parented me for decades; these past few weeks I parented her. Who knows, maybe someday my kids will return that same favor.

As much as I hope years from now they have happy thoughts of their Grammy, it's a spectacular thing to know pictures and videos of them being loved by her, from the day they were born up until last week, flood our home.

Whether they actually *remember* my Mom or not, she'll never be forgotten.

# JUNE

## Muttin' But Love

Six weeks since Mom died.

That has nothing in particular to do with this month—it certainly doesn't have anything to do with the story about a mechanical dinosaur that I sat down here to try to write and the letter I just went to the post office to send—but the timeline of how many days since I last saw her is top of mind, suffocating every move I make. That first sentence unexpectedly fell out of me.

But Mutt. The dinosaur. Let me try to write a normal story. Every day in public I create an outward appearance, smiling-smiling-smiling, while inside I feel like a ball of flooded thoughts, so let me try it here on a keyboard as well.

ఇ౩౮౦

Parker continues to write letters to Mutt, a statue at the North
Carolina Zoo. I continue to mail her creatively decorated notes to
Wes's mom—Parker's Zizi—who replies as if she's this imaginary
animal. Parker was four years old when we took her to Asheboro
and she "met" Mutt. In her imagination-packed mind, she decided
the huge display was her real-life friend.

Two years later, she is still in total belief. I find it a better storyline
than Santa. Please note the plant food Parker put on the envelope

she sent to this pretend herbivore. Zina, who works at the post
office, watched me package all this up today. She says she follows
these adventures of Parker and Hutch, and can't believe Parker still

writes to Mutt. She insisted I document and share the fact Mutt lives on. I told her I would, if she let me take her picture to show her off, too.

Zina's right. It is a good smiling story. A typical keep-your-mind-moving-daily-little-smiling story. Something to help keep the deeper "I can't believe it's been six weeks and one day" thoughts down to a small place.

---

*COMMENTS:*

**Linda P.** I love Parker and her antics. And, grief takes time.

**Joy W.** The minds of little ones. My 4-year-old grandbaby Raven watches the show *Mountain Monsters* and swears to everyone that Big Foot lives in the woods behind our house. She has seen him, heard him and he growls/yells and then speaks Spanish.

**Glenn H.** Your daughter may be the first young lady I've heard of who likes a dinosaur. Let thoughts be. You have them because they're there.

## MONTH THIRTY-TWO: Sleepless in Charlotte

6:09 a.m.: I've been up since 5:03 a.m. and am desperate. I wouldn't unleash this devilish little nugget upon my worst enemy.

The black bags underneath my eyes the last many weeks—thank you to the three viewers who have pointed them out in emails—must be permanent. Hutch, a perfect eater and sleeper for the first thirty months of his life, gave up sleeping two months ago.

There's too much going on to try to parent. When he's woken up long before the crack of dawn, I've let him get up and start his day. Big mistake. Huge mistake, actually. That nondealing way to deal has led to where I am right now: crouching in a playroom, typing one-handed on my phone, aimlessly moving a toy car back and forth and back and forth and back and forth with my left hand, pretending to enjoy playing "speedway" with Hutch as he makes *vroom-vroom* noises around me. He is wide, wide awake. I'll do anything I can do to keep him entertained and not go wake up his sister. No one likes double trouble.

11:13 a.m.: I am on coffee cup four. This is not a joke. I'm hitting reply to the note I typed myself this morning so I can keep my daily log today all in one place. I don't even know why. Just feels like I should. Maybe I'll write again later.

12:30 p.m.: Parker is enjoying her last day of school, so I'm taking this opportunity to try to have a civilized conversation with Hutch about his amazing bed and why he should stay in it overnight. We're in his room. Because this is normal, right? This is what experts say to do? To talk with your child and REASONABLY explain why things should be the way they need to be?

So here I am, explaining the need to stay in his own room and how he is no longer allowed to get up before the sun is awake.

He is fiddling with his new shark sandals and asking if we can go to Chick-fil-A.

Pep talk over.

1:16 p.m.: Help. Drowning. I need a ring buoy tossed out with a solution about how to make a mobile child stay in his (or her) new "big kid" bed. This general thought about his nighttime sleep schedule clouds everything in my life, even during the afternoon. I'm getting ready for work as I text this to myself. I should have no time for these added thoughts. I'm heading to interview the mayor today and anchor four shows, yet this is the only question in my muddled mind.

Before you suggest whatever you're about to suggest, here's how we got to where we are:

- Hutch started cannonballing off his crib in mid-April.
- After a few days of watching this on repeat through a baby monitor, I felt certain he was going to crack his head open.
- Wes dusted off Parker's old big-kid bed gathering cobwebs in a shed.
- We told Hutch it was his.
- Oh, the excitement!
- He jumped around and showed off his dance moves.
- Then he put books and toys in it "to decorate."
- He then lay down and said, "Hutch bed! Hutch bed!"
- Total ownership.
- Voilà. Done. Perfect.

Only not at all. On Night One he stayed in the bed for an hour. With no crib-like obstacles and full access to open air, he went through each toy basket in his room in the shadow of his night-light. (I know this because everything was overturned the next morning.) Eventually, he opened his bedroom door, walked down the hall, and woke me up. I took him back to his room. He came back. I took him back to his room. He came back. I finally dragged him into bed with me.

That went on repeat three nights in a row until Google gave me a brilliant solution: Get a tent!

By Night Four, Hutch's new bed had this red *Cars* thing on top. It was supposed to—Google said—make him feel more enclosed and less likely to climb out.

Didn't work. Nothing has worked.

We're now at the stage where Hutch will sleep until 3a.m.-ish, then wander down the hall . . . just because he can. I'll have only recently gotten home from work myself to fall asleep, so he knows I'm the more likely candidate to wake up faster. Without talking, I put him back in his own bed. Sometimes I even lie with him on that teeny kid mattress. Other times I shut the door and guard it on the outside so when he gets up and opens it, I'm standing there with arms crossed. He hears me say a firm "Go back." He turns around, and once in the tent, I'll shut the door. But he's patient. Calculating. I'll wait outside that door for TwentyLongForever minutes, and the first moment I finally think we're good and I return to my room, he suddenly appears at my side.

We do this dance every night.

When he does finally fall asleep—sometimes with me on the hallway carpet outside his door—he then wakes up for good around 5:30 a.m. When he was in a crib he slept like clockwork until 7:30 a.m.

What's a parent who doesn't get home until 1 a.m. every night to do? How do you train children to stay asleep?

2:12 p.m.: I'm now at work, riding shotgun in a live truck, heading to the mayor's office, and re-read that stream of consciousness. I'd like to add that I'm open to any idea except dragging heavy furniture outside his door and barricading him inside because A) that sounds slightly abusive and mentally harmful and B) I've looked into it and it's a fire hazard.

4:52 p.m.: Back in the newsroom. Heading to set to do first show of the day. Want to add this fact: I'm a fan of letting babies "cry it out." As infants, Parker and Hutch both quickly learned that bedtime was bedtime, and when they went down, they weren't getting back up until the sun rose in the morning. Didn't matter how long they cried. They got it. This rebelling from Hutch is *all new*.

8:38 p.m.: Three shows down and a follow-up thank-you to the interview done, I went home and put kids down and grabbed dinner. I've switched to caffeinated tea.

Please, when you see bags under my eyes at 11 p.m., lie through the keyboard and tell me they're pretty.

---

*COMMENTS:*

**Terry B.** I found out too late that the best way around these problems is to skip having children and move right to grandkids. With grandkids, you can always return them to their parents when they get too rowdy.

**Christine G.** Three nights. Every time he gets up you put him back. No hugs, no talk (minimal just to say back to bed calmly), just put him back. Your arms will fall off. Your back will hurt. You and everyone around you will be miserable. But it WILL work.

**Michelle P.** Glow in the dark stickers. If he stays in his big boy bed all night, then he gets glow in the dark stickers to put on his pajamas the next night. It worked wonders for my little one twenty something years ago.

**Brenda B.** The bags show humanity.

**Erin W.** We went through the same thing, but mine didn't even come close to making it to 3 a.m. He would go to sleep with me on the floor beside his bed, and the exact second my foot would step outside his door, he'd wake up and get up. I don't know how he knew.

**Annie E.** Reading this as I put my 3-year-old back in his big boy bed for the 30th time.

**Kim G.** I read your posts about Hutch and I swear I am like, "Molly is spying on me and my boy Rhett." I just give in and let him crawl in bed with me because we all are better people in the morning when we have adequate sleep. I am sure I will probably grow to regret this decision but for now it keeps me from turning into a complete zombie.

**Rodney E.** Rum and coke over ice. (Just kidding for those about to freak out.)

**Annette Mc.** If you find something that works, please patent it.

# JULY

## Where Is My Baby Girl?

First day of two-year-old summer school for an apprehensive Hutch, and it's Parker who takes his hand and lunchbox, leads the way, introduces him to his teacher (her old one), hugs him goodbye, and tells him we'll see him this afternoon.

---

*COMMENTS:*

**John L.** She's definitely an old soul.

**Eric U.** Not old, just confident.

**Mary J.** How stinking cute, Mini Molly.

## Five Angels

People write often about waves. How they reflect the ups and downs of life. What strikes me as I sit staring at the ocean is their consistency. They are infinite. They rolled in at the beginning of time and will presumably roll until the end. They change in form—big or small, rough or calm—but they never go away. I can drink them in with my eyes, and little by little their never-ending pattern washes away hard-edged thoughts.

Waves are a free hypnotic therapy the world has gifted us all.

That's my first thought about this weekend:

The beach is a perfect place to send someone home.

It took a few days to process the other thoughts. From her perch high above, I know my mom saw our celebration. She must know it captured the essence of *her*. She was an artist who always visualized, and never needed things to be laid out directly. But I am more linear. I like putting things on the record. Which means I feel compelled to actually say:

It was everything she would've wanted.

Twenty-nine people, some who had never met, together for three days. She was the center of attention, the common thread, and would've adored seeing cousins she had grown up with from birth meet friends she had as an adult.

It was a little hippie (Parker gets it honestly), a little random, fully loving, and a life moment for us all. That group of us will most likely never be in the same place again, but we had this past weekend to touch us in different ways to take back home.

I could post a dozen pictures, but in some ways the one here of five female backs says it all.

These are the five "Angels" my mom named before she passed. Before she slipped into her coma, she told me to contact them and tell them they were the five women in her life who in different times carried her through. They were all honored . . . and a bit  surprised. These five ladies showed up to Kure Beach, along with my mom's brothers and nieces and nephews, and the twenty-nine of us together honored mom's spirit two months after her body had left.

I can tell you this much: when it's my time, I know how I'd like to go. How fantastic it must be to float above and see everyone you love at a beach, showing videos, swapping memories, shedding tears, and forging friendships.

Thank you to the many who have sent messages and asked questions. My mom was an open book who shared her breast-cancer battle with the world, something easy to appreciate. But now, I say softly, it's done. I want to keep the memories from this past weekend alive in my own head and heart and start to move forward.

With that said, I'm going to try to look ahead. Actually, really, give it dedicated effort, and try. Many thoughts of her and death and hospice have consumed my past two months. I'm a decent enough actress to get through the motions of a day with no one really knowing the mental reality behind it all. And for this, I'm grateful. But now is the time to look toward the future.

I still have hatred for cancer. I still think we need to find a damn cure. I'm still on board with fighting to make that happen. Now though, as I step forward, this picture of the Angels will be my tangible motivation.

I've been typing for thirty minutes, looked up, and saw the waves. They never stopped.

Mom is at peace.

*COMMENTS:*

**Cindi W.** Today is the 8th anniversary of my mom's passing from cancer. Perfect time to read this post. I think all those cancer-free ladies are having their own celebration in heaven.

**Tammy T.** I couldn't think of a better way to be remembered. The beach is medicine.

**Vickie G.** Cathartic.

**Elizabeth B.** What a beautiful tribute to your mother. I am a 7-year breast cancer survivor. Was doing chemo for my first Komen "Race for the Cure" and had to be pushed in a wheelchair, was too weak to walk. The picture was the following year. Hope to be there again this year.

**Ann B.** I lost my mom 7 years ago. It gets easier. I'm not really sure why since she was my best friend and I miss her more than anything. But I know she wouldn't want me to be sad. I feel like she is right there with me when I go to the beach and hear waves.

**Carolyn L.** It is a wonderful thing for women to have other women in their life. There are times we feel we couldn't make it without them. We should always pay it forward in a sisterhood.

**Brian C.** This hits home. This damn dreaded disease.

## MONTH THIRTY-THREE:
### Meet iPhone, the Babysitter

If given the chance, Hutch would have his face five inches from a screen every waking minute of his life. He is obsessed. In either a very sad commentary about the parenting he receives, or a sign of true toddler brilliance—I can't decide which—he knows how to navigate a smartphone better than most adults.

Ask my friend Angie.

The other day she offered to jump in and watch both Parker and Hutch at her home. She had them playing in the lake behind her house, riding a boat, and eating fluffernutter sandwiches.

Throughout all the fun, Hutch continued to ask (politely, she said) for her phone. At some point, hours into the enjoyment and back inside, she finally let him hold it. He apparently said thank you and waddled into the other room.

*He is two*, she thought. *What could he actually do on my phone?* Mm-hmm.

After ten quiet minutes, she says she saw the back of Hutch's towhead looking down as he sat comfortably among her couch pillows. She sent her older son to check on him.

He came back laughing.

"Mom," he said. "Hutch found and downloaded Kids YouTube."

C3**80

Later that night Angie got a call from her boss. He doesn't usually call her at night, so she was a bit confused. Especially when he said he'd called that afternoon and "a baby picked up."

*What?*

"When I asked if you were there, the baby said, 'Mama's phone,'" Angie's boss told her. "Then the baby hung up on me."

"I'm sorry," Angie said. "You should've tried calling back."

"I did!" Her boss laughed. "That little boy did the same thing to me again. Said he was watching *Peppa Pig*. Who is Peppa Pig?"

CR**80

Most parents have rules about screen time. I've taken polls of friends, and all households differ. Our house has screen rules, too. But this summer they've gone slack. I won't waste your time with the excuses why; bottom line, when Hutch gets restless and I'm exhausted, or he's up at the crack of dawn and I want to sleep another hour, I hand him my phone.

Those facts don't make me proud, but there is no use sugarcoating. Truth is, I don't know how to parent iPhone/iPad screen time.

I am good on limiting TV, but that's because I was raised watching limited TV. Every weekday at 4 p.m., my mom let me pull my kiddie chair to the one television we had in the house and glue my eyes to *Sesame Street*. She called it "her hour of peace." Afterward, the TV was turned back off. I didn't whine for more. I didn't really care.

Therefore, limiting Parker and Hutch on cartoons has been easy: one or two in the morning, and one or two at night. That's it. She's fine. He's fine. I parent the way I was raised. All is well.

But we didn't have rules for smartphones when I was growing up.

There were no YouTube channels.

Handheld gadgets didn't talk back.

Touch screens weren't existent.

Those are things Hutch now wants, and I don't have a natural base from which to start.

Websites everywhere will tell you what's proper and appropriate, with scientific quotes from childhood "experts." I have friends who enforce strict rules about only watching screens on weekends. I have other friends who hand their babies expensive smartphones any time of day, in any public place, without any concern whatsoever.

There are conflicting messages everywhere you turn. I don't know how much screen time is too much, but I know Hutch would hold the phone all day if I'd let him. He loves the engagement. He loves ABCmouse (an educational preschool app). He'll look endlessly at pictures and videos of family members.

And let's face it—it's EASY. If I need to check emails, clean up a room, work on a project, or just keep him in one place where he won't run into trouble, handing him my phone is a sure way to give myself an uninterrupted ten minutes.

Is that so bad? He still seems social and happy. His eyesight is normal. I listen to those educational phone programs teach letters of the alphabet. I smile when I hear him laugh out loud as he watches videos of himself.

I have no problem being a tough mom and letting him throw a tantrum when I keep the phone away. But I'm also guilty of handing it over to give myself a break.

Toughest part is . . . as soon as I figure out how to perfectly parent this phone preoccupation, there will be new technology and new lines to attempt to draw.

*COMMENTS:*

**Vicki F.** Thanks for being open. My 3-year-old grandson is just like Hutch and every other toddler in this day and time of technology. If we use some sense and let them also play outside and do other things, I say no big deal.

**Christine M.** Before I had my daughter I'd say, "I'll NEVER let the TV babysit my child(ren)!" Then I had my daughter and I'd need to do something quickly and by myself, like just go pee. I often think back to that very silly, naive self and laugh.

**Wendy M.** I think they come out of the womb these days knowing how to navigate those devices.

**Emily D.** Who CARES about the "rules?" Your kids, your decisions.

**Chelse P.** There are always perfect parents who know everything. I love when people are completely honest. My kid gets too much "screen time." Oh well. It'll all be okay.

**Brandy R.** Heaven knows we all harbor mom guilt.

# AUGUST

## Morning Rituals

---

*COMMENTS:*

**Tim S.** I thought he got a haircut.

 **Molly.** He did. It grows.

**JDarlene B.** My Monday morning ritual, driving an hour-and-a-half to come to Charlotte to watch this one.

**Todd C.** Working on that 3:00 shadow.

**Jeff J.** #HutchFuzz

## MONTH THIRTY-FOUR:
### The Summer of Copycat

Oh, I'm so very late with this monthly post. I meant to write around the second week of the month, as would be normal, then something happened, then another thing, then this stuff and that stuff, and add it up and here we are late August.

There were just way too many fantastic memories for the digital scrapbook. Eventually it became a decision I didn't want to have to make: which one story should I document when all were excellent, but none seemed an obvious choice?

Should I write about Parker's dentist appointment (her ability to dramatically showcase a story, even while lying down, mouth wide open, staring at the dental tech, unable to speak but still inexplicably and effectively "on stage"), or do I write about Disney's *Descendants* (which has taken over our lives)? There is the issue of Hutch and high heels that needs to be remembered, and also that nagging confession about how I'm dying for school to start PleaseRightNow because TheKidsAreDrivingMeNuts.

Each day I waited to write, something else would pile on the mental mountains . . . another file folder added to the always-open brain cabinets.

August was about to wrap, with no monthly memory on record, when suddenly this video of the kids dancing resurfaced. It was taken weeks ago at Kure, rediscovered by Hutch this morning. The two-year-old iPhone master found it as he cruised through camera archives.

"Mama! I danceeeng with my seeester!"

I went over and watched with him. Then watched again. He kept hitting play, loving seeing himself shun Parker as she tried to teach him moves. They had live music and an empty stage at an outdoor restaurant, and as soon as she turned her back, he started to twirl just like her.

On the fifth time Hutch and I watched this little clip together, it hit me: this thirty-second video represents our entire summer, a perfect visual metaphor of how the end of this season should be remembered.

It shows how Parker has gotten more mature and independent. And Hutch, who has always been a quieter, funnier, more easygoing "roll with it" child, has watched her every single move with absorbing eyes and now wants to be exactly like her, while simultaneously trying to still be himself.

The hidden messaging in the video screams like a neon sign

to me. She reaches for him in the beginning—which she always does—but he then shoos her away. If his arms could talk, they'd be screaming, "I can do it myself!" (That's typical. Because he's had her in his face for thirty-four months of life, he has learned to react the exact way she reacts, and "I can do it myself!" is classic Parker.)

In response she shrugs—total her—and spins on.

He thinks twice as he watches her move away. Then he starts to do what she does, but . . .

. . . in his own way, to his own beat . . .

. . . without wanting her to hover . . .

. . . declaring independence while copying her every move.

That whole sequence is the key to understanding their relationship: he can't live without her, but doesn't want her to know how much he needs her around. (To see the video go to http://tinyurl.com/BlogMonth34)

There are other examples, too. From this month specifically:

- If she orders ice cream first, he wants the exact flavor she just said. Then he'll sit right next to her and eat his cone in a different direction, maybe starting at the bottom if she's starting at the top.
- If she is playing on the playset, he wants to play on the playset, too . . . but a different section. If she's on the swing, he wants the slide. He's copying her, while trying to show he's not her.

• If she's practicing reading with her finger on the page, tracing words down the line in the sentence, he'll get out a book, sit nearby, and put his finger on any open page and start saying gibberish. He thinks he's reading just like her, but his own book.

Maybe the most telling example is the hardest part of any given day this summer . . . when she goes off on her scooter down the street to play with neighborhood friends. He can't go. He's too young. It breaks his tiny heart to watch her leave without him. His big blue ocean eyes tear up with sincere, devastated sadness. Takes him a good ten minutes to recover and find something to do with only Mommy or Daddy, and not her.

Watching him cry as she speeds down the sidewalk shatters my heart, too.

Month Thirty-Four, you came to me in an absolute perfectly accidental form to reflect the truth of what recently emerged: a little brother's adoration for his older sister, shown in how he emulates her every move, all while not wanting her to know he's watching.

Infatuation. Expressed by imitation. Laced with independence.

Love, pure and simple.

*COMMENTS:*

**Randy F.** We feel almost like family keeping up with their growing pains. Reminds me so much of raising my own kids.

**Fran G.** These stories are childhoods in a nutshell. Dancing to the music in their heads, eating sand, and pitching a fit for a little black dress. I remember that story from your first book so well.

**Kathi A.** Without watching the video, I could see it happening between them with words.

**Susan W.** Read this with a tear in my eye envisioning my two grown men sons as little boys.

**Jan T.** I called mine Pete and Repeat when they were those ages.

# SEPTEMBER

## MONTH THIRTY-FIVE: The Day the Dress Died

My hippie princess is no longer in dresses. God, that's hard to write.

The first day of school she was still in love with flowy skirts. She changed from one dress to another as she got ready. Couldn't decide which was best. But the next morning she woke up and came downstairs in what you see here. I snapped this photo at the bus stop that second day, thinking I'd be noting the first and only day of her childhood she didn't wear a dress.

Little did I know I was noting a shift in identity.

Dresses were all Parker has gravitated toward since she was old enough to form an opinion (which was quite young). As an eighteen-month-old, she'd kick out her legs on the changing table, refusing any attempt I made to put on a onesie. The first time she went to soccer practice, she wore a tutu on the field. At kindergarten gym class, she wore a skirt and sneakers. Her roller-skating sixth birthday party was a long dress with rented skates. Every outfit she picked out in a store was something with a skirt. Every Halloween costume was a gown. Every kids' clothing catalog we received had dog-eared pages on only dresses.

Up until the moment you see here, she was a fearless first grader who had never worn pants.

She had three pairs of leggings in her closet that I got for her when we were back-to-school shopping this year at Marshalls. You're staring at one of them. The other two were black. I picked them up thinking they could be like tights when it got cold.

She has gone back and forth between wearing those three pairs of leggings almost every day this past month.

To be clear, whatever Parker wants to wear she can wear, assuming it's appropriate. Leggings, dresses, skirts, sneakers with a ball gown, dressy shoes with jeans, whatever. She can find her own style. We welcome her to do so.

But it makes me sad she isn't drawn to dresses anymore. Her closet currently has new unworn ones from that shopping trip. Meantime, the three leggings are worn through with holes in multiple spots.

Since taking this picture—by the way, this shirt reads "Everybody Loves a Big Sister"—she has donned some of her favorite older dresses on days all three leggings are in the laundry. So it's not a *refusal* to wear them, just a clear, sudden, immediate shift in how she wants to present herself. She wants to evolve in a visible way. Take a vacation from all she's ever known.

Hmm . . .

I'm sitting here writing this . . . thinking . . . knowing . . . realizing?? . . .

She's growing up.

Maturity can show itself in peculiar, unexpected ways.

I know I've said this before, but her leaps forward are even more evident this month. Other moments were subtle, but this clothes thing is the biggest slap in the face. Less obvious examples include:

- Never forgets her helmet when she rides her scooter down the street to a friend's house. Understands safety rules. More importantly, wants to abide by them.
- I've stood at the end of the driveway watching her hair fly behind her . . . thinking how odd it was that she was old enough to go six houses away, alone.
- We implemented a simple morning chore chart. She wants to get up and accomplish the items. Does it all on her own.
- She likes ballet, but said she also wanted to take hip-hop. Last week she started. Walked into a class of six-and-seven-year-old girls. Didn't act intimidated that she didn't know them.

- We went to Atlanta this weekend to visit my brother's family. Driving home, she *asked* to start on homework. I turned around to see her working on a beanbag lap table, writing spelling words. It transported me twelve years ahead, like we were dropping her off at college. (She later whined about a treat, so a *glimpse* into maturity, not a fully open window.)
- This month she started asking more in-depth questions: "What is divorce?" "If Grammy is in heaven, does she have a brain?" "How do you choose who you marry?"

Her more multi-layered thoughts stump me more and more.

It's crazy that Parker switching her style brings quiet analysis in me. Guess that's parenthood, though—trying to figure out why your child is doing what they're doing, without seeming like you're prying or, in some cases, even noticing.

---

*COMMENTS:*

**Tonya S.** I have a similar dress-wearer who gravitated away from dresses for a short spell. But 8th grade . . . still wearing the most exceptionally frilly dresses she can find to middle school. Many kids are unkind about her outfit choices. And sometimes as much as I'd like her to blend in to keep the bullies away, I still encourage her to be her. Dresses it is. PS: I wouldn't take them out of her closet just yet.

**Betty N.** Self-confidence is sooooo important. I still struggle with it. May she retain it forever.

 **Molly.** Confidence can be fragile. For all ages.

**Caroline P.** My oldest daughter is 12 and has begun changing so much recently. It seems like overnight there is something new about her. I see the young woman she is becoming and it both takes my breath away and breaks my heart. Time flies.

**Elisha J.** First grade is a big year for growing and changing. I teach first graders—just wait until after Christmas. You can tell they really grow and bloom.

**Jane P.** Better get back to Marshalls.

**Chante B.** My daughters both went through all about wearing dresses to none. They have both went back to dresses in their own time. My youngest loves to help me do renovations around the house. This is her in a brand new dress helping mix mortar, lay tile, and using a power drill and hammer.

**Mary Katherine S.** I wore a dress every day in kindergarten and then stopped. My 1st grade teacher was so disappointed—she only had boys and had loved seeing my dresses.

**Jennifer H.** #PrincessInPants

## Abby's Flower Girl

Abby is Wes's first cousin. They grew up together in Louisville, Kentucky. She's remarkably artistic, kind, and really excited to get married this weekend. Parker is her flower girl. She adores Abby and can't wait to be part of her wedding.

After getting engaged, Abby was diagnosed with breast cancer. It was a stunning diagnosis to our entire family. At only twenty-five years old, Abby has gone through her journey with a level of grace that's hard to describe. She talks with a smile, always, about the family and her job and friends and soon-to-be husband Adam. She doesn't harp on the hand she was dealt, but posts happy pictures of herself in scarves, cheers everyone else on, and laughs every fifth sentence.

Abby's mom, Aunt Suzi, has helped Abby tackle the journey head-on, and I have been in awe of their strength. Adam also shaved his head in solidarity.

All this to say, Abby . . . we love you. So much. I'm sitting at work, staring at this photo from the summer, 1000 percent distracted, wanting to get home to pack and hop on a plane to see you. We want to celebrate YOU. Everyone who knows you does. Your weekend is here. Finally! How awesome it will all be.

PS: Quick warning: Parker already told me "Flower girls wear makeup." Get ready.

---

*COMMENTS:*

**Abby S.** I love this message, and can't wait to see all of you guys. She'll be a great flower girl. It will be an amazing weekend.

**Beth F.** Parker sure is blessed to be surrounded by AMAZING, strong, gorgeous women! You, your Mom, Abby, and I'm sure there are plenty more. Best wishes for a beautiful wedding weekend, Abby, and a life full of joy, laughter, and love.

**Dee L.** How wonderful to see the giant smiles of these two.

**Angel M.** Makeup it is, Parker. A girl who knows what she likes.

**Krezen G.** Can't wait to see pictures! Abby and Parker are so cute together!

 **Molly.** Stay tuned . . .

# OCTOBER

## Mom Didn't Matter

The most glowing bride, a new husband proud to claim his spot beside her, and a flower girl who didn't let them alone the whole night. It would've been embarrassing—who wants a six-year-old attached to their hips, in their arms, holding their hands every minute on their big day? Not many brides. But oh, Abby and Adam welcomed her. Never batted an eyelash. Invited her along every step of the way. They even got introduced at the reception as Mr. and Mrs. with Parker walking in alongside them.

The pictures are priceless. Parker cried when she realized her assigned dinner plate was beside me and not at the head table with "the girls." When the bridesmaids gave her a wink and waved her over, she grabbed her china place setting (specially ordered chicken fingers and fries) and set up shop beside them in a seat they created. She tore up the dance floor all evening, and knew every groomsman by the end of the night. Got her picture with every last cute one of them. I was left in the dust. She even asked the bridesmaids to go with her when she needed to find a potty and—apologies to the vendor—learned how to use the group photo booth better than the man hired to run it. I watched from afar, wondering how I'd eventually get her to come down from the pedestal on which she was perched.

She was on fire until midnight, when her sweet bobby-pinned, wispy-haired head was so heavy she leaned into me and Wes as we walked to the hotel. She asked me to help take off her new bracelet, unzip her dress, and rub her feet, because her "princess shoes" gave her a blister. She eventually fell asleep with one arm around Brown Bear and the other holding my hand. I was back. Mommy was back.

It's amazing how a six-year-old can appear sixteen, but at the end of the day, she's still just your baby.

---

*COMMENTS:*

**Stephen Mc.** Careful, Parker. Not polite to outshine the bride.

 **Molly.** Nobody was going to outshine Abby. It was her night.

**Nancy P.** Just give it a little bit of time. Little brother will do the job of knocking her off that pedestal.

## MONTH THIRTY-SIX: Turning Three

Dear Hutch,

I woke up in the wee hours and felt compelled to write you a love letter. It sounds crazy—later in life, you can laugh at me—but I wrote one to your sister a couple years ago and was gripped with this 3 a.m. sensation that you would someday grow up and read hers and wonder why you didn't have one. So here we are. A love letter from me to you.

Happy birthday, my little nugget.

Three years ago we were in the hospital. You were eight days late and perfectly content to stay where you were. Eventually you greeted us, October 11, with barely a cry. I don't have a ton of memories from your first few days . . . everything was a whirlwind . . . but I do remember your easygoing joy. At just a few days old, you were happy to lie in anyone's arms as long as you were fed.

Lots of things have changed in three years, though your love of food remains.

I took this picture yesterday of you sneaking into the pantry. One of your favorite things to do is dive your hand directly into the peanut butter. The second you heard me call your name from behind your back (with my phone ready to capture your reaction), you knew you were caught.

You turned slowly. You weren't startled. I made an instant mental note about your composure. Even though you were found with your hand around the figurative cookie jar, you didn't drop the food or start to whine or even try to hide your mischief, which would be the gut reaction for many kids. Instead, you gripped the peanut butter harder and turned to look at me from the corner of your eyes. You have grit, Hutch. I'm convinced you know how powerless I am when you shift your eyes to the side and smile slightly to give me a devilish squint. It was perfectly played.

I laughed. I couldn't help it. I laughed because you doubled down and dug your heels in deeper, unapologetically owning your wrong.

Speaking of heels . . .

These cowboy boots. Lawd help me, I'm in deep love with how much you love your cowboy boots. You picked them out yourself and demand to wear them with jeans, gym shorts, or pajamas. The knowledge of what it feels like to help smush your feet and little toes into them is ingrained in me forever, but watching you walk once they're on is what gets me the most. You start on the heel and rock forward. Serious three-year-old swagger.

And of course, when you're wearing them, everyone stops to tell you how cute you look. People—friends, strangers, whoever—get down to your eye level, and use sweet words that your ears eat up. You relish attention.

Which is okay. Most people like a little attention.

What else do you love? Ninja Turtles. Any edible item on someone else's dinner plate. The ringing cash register in the playroom. An iPhone and Kids YouTube, which you call "KidsTube." You love your sister's necklaces, my super-high heels, and car keys. You'll sit in a driver's seat of any vehicle for hours and mess with side-view mirrors, seat-recline buttons, and turn signals. You get fixated on gadgets and how things work. You make us crazy with how many times you repeat the question "Why?"

Recently, you've become obsessed with "Mommy's work" and "Mommy's work pass," the security cards an employee waves at a gate to get into a building. It's pure madness how much you talk about these passes. You even rattled on to my coworkers about their work passes the other day when you visited the station. One of them then awesomely surprised you with a legitimate WBTV News "Hutch" pass, as an early birthday present.

You've held onto it all weekend. I think it makes you feel special to have something Parker doesn't.

What else do I love? How you dance with your whole body and laugh loudly at your moving reflection in a mirror. That you run fast. How you like turning the pages of a book yourself, and don't like being alone. You are oddly neat, often throwing out your own trash and sometimes helping me organize a room. I crack up every time we drive around with Kidz Bop blaring, and your toddler voice blurts out the last two words of each sentence in every refrain.

All good things to record for posterity. All true.

But none of what I just listed conveys how cuddly you are.

You are the most loving child in the world.

You put your arms around everyone you know.

It's beautiful to see your trust in humanity, which might be peculiar to say because you're only three, but we all see children who hang on their parents' legs and don't want to meet new people. I am constantly amazed that as long as you see someone you love hugging someone you don't know, you are fine to hug them too. You are quiet, but never shy.

Of all the people in the world you love, Parker is your favorite. You want her to be proud of you even more than you need my approval. You show Parker your artwork from preschool. You copy her moves on a playground. You won't even let her board the school bus until you give her a huge hug and kiss, as the driver waits with those big yellow doors open and lots of kids stare down from the windows.

She lets you adore her. She loves you that much back.

Hutch, it's now 4 a.m., and I've been typing in a daze for about an hour. You'll be running in wide awake by 6 a.m., maybe 6:30, asking me about my "work pass" while carrying your new one that you fell asleep with last night. I'll get up and we'll start the day, open a couple presents and have Dunkin Donuts as a birthday breakfast treat. I'll re-read all this at some point and maybe wonder if I sound sappy.

I don't care if I do. I love every ounce of your roly-poly being. Your stubbornness, the fact that you're a ham, your ability to adapt, and how much you want to repeatedly kiss my face before I head to work every day. You're the most unique three-year-old boy I know, and I am the most proud woman in the world to say I'm your mom.

Love you, Hutch-man. Happy birthday.

—Mama

---

*COMMENTS:*

**Mandi M.** I can't even believe he's 3! I remember you emceeing Race for the Cure that day, one-day overdue, majorly pregnant, and hoping Hutch held out until the Race was over . . . but it was good to have your doctor there just in case! #AlwaysTeamMolly

**Babby S.** [Preschool Principal] Beautiful words for a precious child. I know he asks me about my work pass about 10 times a day. Love that boy.

**Summer C.** One day your kids will cherish all these sweet moments you write about. I am a single mom of two grown children and in my first year of an empty nest and really wish I'd have written much more down.

 **Molly.** Start writing now. About not having them around. Why not? You can write anything for yourself.

**Patrick G.** I'm a believer that letters, not emails, are one of the best ways to convey our belief, support, admiration, fascination, affection, and appreciation for our kids. I started doing it in grad school when my kids were in their teens. My neighbor died unexpectedly 4 days after retirement when he was 65 and had written letters to his kids and had them in a strong box for when he passed. They read them at the funeral. Extremely touching and his kids will NEVER forget or let them go. The "written word" is severely underrated, but we don't realize that until it is too late.

**Mary Ann B-L.** Since they were born I have kept a journal for my grandchildren who are now 14 and 18. They both love for me to read to them about all the things they did and the funny things they said when they were little. Brings back such sweet memories I get a good chuckle and sometimes a tear as I read the way they were.

**Scott J.** Dammit . . . made me cry . . . with joy and admiration. Nothing like a mother's love. Nothing.

**Mandy M.** Cowboy boots go with every outfit.

## October 31

She's full of tricks. He always wants treats. Happy Halloween.

*COMMENTS:*

**Ernie C.** What costume did you wear for trick or treating Molly?

 **Molly.** A mom on dinner break.

**Barbara D.** I have Harry Hook to go with your Mal! He didn't want to wear Harry's hat, so we improvised.

**Melissa D.** My daughter went as Uma!

**Amy Z.** Molly, I think our daughters had the same idea. This is my little girl with her brother.

**Susan W-Y.** My Superhero:

# NOVEMBER

## End of Soccer Season

When you're a mom who works nights, you miss things. You miss a lot of things. I've learned to be okay with it: Parker and Hutch don't know anything different and always seem to understand.

Tonight was one of those nights. I missed most of Parker's end-of-season soccer party. When I arrived very late, the other parents happily relayed that Parker was given the Swiss Army Knife Award.

Hmmmm?

When she later ran by for a quick hug, I asked. "Why did you get the Swiss Army Knife, P?"

She looked at me. Dead on. Didn't crack a smile. Stared like I was crazy for not knowing. Her answer is why I write this now. I need it to be recorded in digital history so if she has future insecure moments, I can point back to her six-year-old self.

Without a bit of sass and full-on straight-ahead nonchalance, she shrugged her shoulders and said without hesitation, "Because I can do it all."

Bam.

Self-worth is golden.

---

*COMMENTS:*

**Sandra W.** There is no glass ceiling in her future.

 **Molly.** I actually thought in the moment . . . should I teach humility? Tell her to be less sure of herself? Then I almost hit me in the face. STOP. Belief in yourself is a gift.

**Sissy H.** Yes, it is. I'm 50 and I still don't always believe in myself.

**Jenny T.** There will be time for a lesson on humility later.

**Candyce McC.** Your 6-year-old could teach this 58-year-old a thing or two.

**Keith L.** Swiss Army Knives come in many sizes.

## MONTH THIRTY-SEVEN: Hutch's Work Pass

Oh, to be inside a toddler's mind. To know why it is they focus on what they focus on. The expensive toy inside a big box, or the box itself? An outfit you love with embroidered details, or the hand-me-down T-shirt with horrifying cartoon characters peeling off? A cool, smart Leapfrog kids iPad that makes noise while teaching the alphabet, or a cheap plastic electronic security pass that beeps at the gate when driving into the parking lot of Mom's work?

Yeah. That last one. That's Hutch. As I wrote in his birthday letter, more now than ever.

He is obsessed with work passes. Key chains are his current second favorite, so if he meets you and asks to look in your purse, that's why. He'll carry a dozen set of keys around with such elation, you'd think he's holding twelve winning PowerBall tickets.

This addiction to identification badges and keys that unlock doors . . . *this* is the memory for Month Thirty-Seven.

When P and H—what Wes and I find ourselves calling them—look back years and years from now, they won't know it was *this month* the first book launched.  They'll just know it was the Month Hutch WORE US OUT on his addiction to Things That Give Access to Locked Places.

There is no accurate way to fully describe the obsession unless you witness his twenty-four-hour laser focus on these two-inch badges that swipe you into buildings. He sleeps with a work pass just like Parker sleeps with Brown Bear. If mine is not available because I'm at work, he'll curl up with his dad's. Or his own.

He has his own. That birthday gift from weeks ago that was made for him with his name and photo. That badge gives him life.

Part of me thinks I should be embarrassed about this peculiar fact about my son, and start justifying why NO! this does not mean anything odd about his psyche missing his parents while they're working!

But the truth is I don't know why he loves them so much. Maybe it is a psychological way to hold on to something that he knows Mommy and Daddy head off to all the time. But I don't think so.

I think he's a well-adjusted and happy three-year-old, who laughs and plays pranks and bursts out in smiles at his own humor on a constant basis. I think he simply likes the noise passes make when they beep in front of a gate.

I'm no childhood expert, so I won't proclaim his grasp on security badges doesn't have deeper meaning . . . I just know he is going on six weeks of everyday obsession. Sometimes every hour. In bad moments, every other minute.

Example A: His preschool teachers say he goes on and on and on about their ID badges.

Example B: My friend Krista. She'll sit on the sideline with him as we watch our daughters play soccer and listen intently as he waxes on about her driver's license, which he thinks is her work pass. He then begs to hold her keys.

Example C: Almost every photo I have of him doing anything in his life the past many weeks includes a badge or lanyard in his hand or around his neck. Like this one. Bus stop. Waving at cars. *"See my pass? I've got a pass! Anyone? See? My pass!"*

Example D: Halloween. Parker was dressed, ready to score gobs of candy from neighbors. He was the cutest white-haired-Spider-Man around and the only child in America that night who didn't care about candy. He asked to go to my work. That

was his dream night. So I took him. My coworkers were accommodating. Please note the pass in his right hand as he's walking into the building gripping my deskmate's hand with his left.

As if we needed more proof, he's potty-training better now, and you know why? Because I got smart. Instead of offering candy—which is what worked for Parker—if he went in the potty successfully, I told him he could go to my work and use my pass to get into the gate.

*He hasn't had an accident in days.* And every time he's done peeing, he stands up from his Elmo potty and yells, "I get Mommy's work pass! I went pee-pee! I get the pass! I get a pass!"

I've headed to work both days this weekend—my two days off—for him to sit in my lap in the driver's seat and repeatedly swipe that pass over the magic box that opens the gate and lets our car through. All as a reward for not pooping himself. We never entered the actual building once.

CR80

Sometimes I put these monthly posts out with some grand lesson on life. There is no lesson this month. I'm not taking anything out of Hutch and his desire to sleep with a badge other than . . . he likes noise? Maybe one day he'll be an engineer? He has unique interests and that's a good thing about his mind?

Who knows? All I know is my work friends are tolerant, he had an atypical Halloween, and by the grace of God, we finally have some incentive for successful toilet training.

I'm going with it. You use what works. And if you see Hutch coming, hide your keys and disguise your work badge, otherwise you'll be there a long while.

---

*COMMENTS:*

**Molly.** Him, swiping the pass on the box that will open the gate.

**Gina M.** I tried SO hard to get Carolinas Healthcare System to print up badges for our kids years ago for this very reason. They declined due to safety. I broke out the Mod Podge and made one myself.

**Punna S.** Whatever makes them happy and momma's life easier.

**Carol L.** No, this would be difficult to make up.

**Stacy W.** The kids beg to use the swiper at school too. It's magic at that age.

**Kathy F.** My 3-year-old son was obsessed with vacuum cleaners. He actually sat on Santa's lap and asked for a bagless upright.

**Nicole R.** Ivy [one of our #MollysKids] was obsessed with the nurses' badges at Levine Children's Hospital. During her last chemo stay they made her one of her own. She loved it so much that they had to make a second one before we left. It even says "Ivy Riddle, M.D." on it, with her picture.

**Anne C.** The things he's choosing have power. Not just anyone can enter.

**Kirk A.** Can't wait to see what happens when he encounters that ATM machine.

**Bobbie S-W.** Simple. He wants a work pass and keys because that's what mommy has. My kids wanted stethoscopes, and hemostats . . . and scissors. (I was an ER nurse.)

## Giving Thanks for Disney

My mind is like the teacup that kept us twirling for four days. A whirlwind Thanksgiving trip to the Most Magical Place on Earth has me grateful, foggy, and happy to be home.

It's a vacation that leaves you needing one. It's America, with every culture colliding. It's tourism, shoulder-to-shoulder, and heavily scheduled wait times. Sprinkle in some overpriced food and it somehow equals a child's intense joy.

Oh, Parker lit up. To realize the authentic Disney castle she took two months to make with Legos was in front of her eyes . . . there's nothing like seeing it in person. And for my little girl, Princess-obsessed since first learning to curtsy in diapers, a child who painstakingly plowed through that 586-page Lego book of instructions and used her own tiny engineer hands to build the 4,080-piece replica, every bit of her breath was taken away. Which then took mine.

This picture is one of my new favorites in life. She turned toward us after getting close to the golden flags and blue turrets and sandy-gray-white brick of the castle, and it was one of those lucky times a cell phone clicks correctly, capturing a childlike reaction to a  larger-than-life moment, the split second it needed to be caught.

For exhausted parents, however, Disney is not that simple. I've decided you need two things to visit:

1) A Plan.

2) Luck.

There are just too many ways to get frustrated if you don't have a bit of a blueprint for the day. And let me be fair—I planned very little. Our secret success weapon was my sister-in-law Amy. We met up with her, my brother Jay, and their two kids on Day Two. In many ways this trip was in honor of my mom, who always wanted holiday family time together. The eight of us stayed in the same resort, and months ago we all leaned on Amy to become our Disney designer.

 It was Amy who checked the app to work around wait times. It was Amy who knew Animal Kingdom was worth a day trip. It was Amy who determined Magic Kingdom would be less crowded the Sunday after Thanksgiving. (To Parker and Hutch's great delight, we hit the Buzz-Lightyear-Laser-Whatever-It-Was-Called ride three times in a row.)

Thank you, Ames.

Number two on the list, luck. Hope to
find some. We did. In a few days of walking
around, we met Ariel, Donald, Goofy, Elena
of Avalor, Cinderella, Daisy Duck, Minnie
Mouse, Pluto, and stumbled into the very best, first spot on the
parade route where Hutch could wave to everyone—Mickey
looked right at him and waved back.

But all of Disney wasn't such an utter delight.

 It didn't help that Hutch used this trip to test the
waters of independence. He kept shaking off my
hand to walk untethered, which meant we moved at
that lovely tortoise pace that three-year-old legs lead.
He wanted to carry his own umbrella when it started
to rain, he demanded his own map to hold (upside down, mind
you), and he insisted he hold his own FastPass. For those who are
Disney-unaware, your Fast Pass is your Golden Ticket. It comes in
the form of a bracelet. It puts you in the front of a line for three
rides—your choice—that you strategically schedule.

If you lose that bracelet, you're done. No sane adult
would give full FastPass responsibility to a three-
year-old. Unless you're us, walking with Hutch. His
shrieks were worse than the stress of trying to keep
tabs on him, keeping tabs on his bracelet.

But the worst was when he locked me out of a toilet stall. We
were right outside Space Mountain. In light of this newfound independence, he demanded "privacy." I didn't even know he knew the

word. No problem—I figured I'd hold the door from the outside. But once on the other side, that crafty little nugget stood up on his tippy-tippy-toes and pushed the silver lock to the left, keeping me out, effectively locking himself in.

He was cackling through the door. The louder he got, the more I wanted to kill him. Right as I was about to send Parker slithering along that filthy bathroom floor to get on his side, I had an idea: it took a minute for the stall beside him to open, but when it did, I stood on that toilet seat—yes I did—and peered over the top so he

couldn't really see me. Then I spoke, with a Star Wars-like raspy sound. His confused head swiveled. My irritation melted. He was drawers down, looking around but not up, trying to find the floating apparition who knew his name.

I gave specific directions. Deep voiced.

"Finish your pee-pee . . . Hutch. Good boy. Now, pull up your Paw Patrol underwear. Yes. Now, pull up your pants. Use both hands. That's right. Now flush. Only once. Stop flushing the toilet, Hutch. I said once. Thank you. Now . . . walk to the bathroom door. Put your hand up, up, up on the shiny lock. Push it toward the wall. No, Hutch, the other way. Yes. Yes. That's the right way. Good. Now step backward so the door can open."

And waiting there on the other side was Parker, laughing like a hyena, thrilled to be in on the joke.

He never did figure it out.

Parker, for her part, had a deep-seated fear of roller coasters,

which turned into a deep fear of everything. Also odd, she wanted to continually
show off mermaid poses for the King
Titan statue.

Besides the individual stories every
family finds, there's the shared joy we all
experience at Disney's brilliance in creating timeless rides. Splash
Mountain was the same huge fun from twenty-five years ago when
it opened. And Tomorrowland was built in 1971, yet still feels like
a version of the future. Parker and Hutch had never heard of Swiss
Family Robinson, but adored the tree house. And all the stereo-
typical imagery and clothing of It's A Small World—which
probably wouldn't fly if built in today's politically correct times—
Disney managed to make seem unifying and beautifully happy.

The best though might be when Hutch met
Minnie Mouse and showed her his WBTV work
pass. He still wears it daily as a prized possession, so
at first I thought nothing about him outstretching
it to show her. But moments after watching Minnie
do nothing, just standing there with that mouse
head and big fluttery eyelashes, Aunt Amy nudged me. I realized
Minnie was looking at us like, "I'm used to autographing books
and selfies. What am I supposed to do with this?"

This was a wonderfully nontraditional Thanksgiving in a nontraditional year. We're grateful. For family, for surprises, and to get on
that plane and head home.

*COMMENTS:*

**Wendy B.** Two children, wiped out after a long day at Animal Kingdom and four straight rides on Everest:

**Wendell C.** You and I could share very similar stories from our week at Disney. So amazing to see everything through my kids' eyes. Exciting, wondrous, exhausting.

**Shawn L.** I've always said Disney should have commercials showing how everyone enters the park holding hands skipping and laughing and the kids are so excited, and then at the end of the day either dead asleep, or having an absolute meltdown because they're so overly tired.

**Betsy T.** I love the "voice of God" story from the bathroom stall. Priceless!

**Eileen F.** The story about the bathroom stall is one of those that will get told over and over at family gatherings, and may even be told at your funeral many years down the road.

**Shelly M.** I know how you feel. We just got home from DW a couple weeks ago and we're still trying to process the 7 days we spent there at ALL the parks! In 5 days I walked 32 miles according to my steps app.
The kids we took ranged from 10–21, but the 2 families that went milked the most fun out of it as we could. Here is a pic of our 7 kids "dressed" as the Seven Dwarfs with Snow White.

**Carla H.** My girls wanted to go the year my oldest graduated from college and my youngest graduated from high school. They had so much fun recreating photos from their childhood trips. It was the best graduation gift for them (and me and their dad). Enjoy every moment. They grow up so fast.

 **Molly.** My boy.

 **Molly.** My girl.

# DECEMBER

## MONTH THIRTY-EIGHT: Changing Traditions

Memories raced in my mind like they were at never-ending swim practice. They blocked any creativity. In the lead, center lane, doing lap after lap after lap, was the thought of this picture.

It's from the last time my mom, Parker, and I went to *The*

*Nutcracker.* We went every year for Christmas. I didn't know how P would handle us going alone this year. It was a concern I couldn't shake starting sometime in September. Just the two of us felt like it would highlight the absence of the third.

Without being able to voice it in any eloquent way, Parker felt the same. As December approached and *Nutcracker* ads started appearing on TV, she asked who we would take, "if Grammy wasn't here." I let it grow into a dilemma. Bigger, probably, than it needed to be. I didn't know what to do.

My good friend Krista (yes, of the soccer sideline passes) saved the day. She gathered a large group of moms and daughters—fifteen of us—to go to *The Nutcracker*, and somehow even magically organized a backstage meet-and-greet with the Sugar Plum Fairy.

It was ideally different. Fresh mixed with comfortable. I thought of my mom that day but didn't feel wistful. Parker laughed with girls her age and got a Clara ornament.

Later she told me she was pretending that ornament was a gift from Grammy.

Silly me. I half-thought her happiness through the afternoon meant she'd forgotten the past three years with three generations in the three seats. Not at all. She was just enjoying the new *while* remembering the old.

That was my first sign this holiday that change can bring joy.

CԹ8Ծ

The second sign came December 25.

My mom adored Christmas and family and wrapping too many presents. She'd give eclectic, random gifts that elicited laughter. She cooked too much, told stories, and decorated everything. She'd always pick a long weekend within three weeks of the actual day and call it "hers" on the calendar—the family would land wherever she was, and all ages would find festivity in her quirky ideas and sentiment.

None of that happened this year. For the first year ever, we didn't travel. Never packed a car or shipped Santa to another state. Maybe next year we'll go back to hectic holiday madness, but this year it felt right to let things sit.

And . . . just like the *Nutcracker* afternoon . . . someone else took over making it unexpectedly special. My brother Warner, who lives in Washington, DC, showed up 7:30 a.m. on Christmas morning. Biggest surprise in the world. He was creeping through our backyard with a sack on his back, an Amazon-bought curly beard covering most of his face, circular thin-wired spectacles on his eyes, and a pillow stuffed in a red-and-white jacket. The kids screamed with joy that Santa Claus was at their house.

I knew that gait anywhere and instinctively screamed his name. "UNCLE WARNER!"

Thank you to the Goddess above who spurred me to grab my phone and snap a few photos in the midst of jumping up and down. The pictures will be printed out and kept forever. My favorite, here.

Joy in change.

Why do I write this? Because it's what I do. It has been hard to write Month Thirty-Eight unsure about the approaching holidays and the old traditions swimming in my mind, images of Mom cluttering other parts of the brain. I felt stuck. Mentally and verbally.

Then this morning, with Christmas officially in the rearview, that center-lane thought suddenly stopped doing laps. It stood up in the shallow end. It might have even knocked on my skull to get attention.

*I'm changing direction*, it calmly told the inside of me. *Traditions don't need to be obstacles to overcome . . . rather, a starting point to build on.*

You know, joy in change. It'd been showing itself in beautiful ways the past few weeks. I just hadn't recognized it until this morning.

I ran to my computer.

Words started flowing.

Here we are.

03൬

This past month had lots of laughs (A new Hutch North Pole work pass continues to be a crack-up) and lots of love. But when looking back years from now, what I want to remember most from this month is how we found new happiness, despite noted absences.

Happy New Year.

*COMMENTS:*

 **Molly.** This year's Nutcracker group photo. Ideally different from last year.

**Mandy M.** I lost my mom this year and this is just what I needed to read this morning. I tried to do Christmas like Mom did, tried to stick with her traditions only to find with her not present it wasn't the same. So, here's to Day One of 365. These words have helped me to start this first day with the right frame of mind.

**Pat A.** To have a brother that thought to do what he did was amazing. Happy New Year.

 **Molly.** Uncle Warner is amazing. So are my other two brothers. I'm a lucky sister.

**Connie B.** I lost my dad in November so the holidays were much different for my family as well. I kinda dreaded Christmas Day, but as we went through it, we shared sweet memories of my sweet Daddy and together made our way, remembering.

**Betsy P.** Lost my mom in 2008. Hanging my 60-year-old knitted stocking (and the others she made), joined by the new family addition of ones I have knitted; eating off her Christmas dishes and "the kids" (now past the age of 30), reading the Christmas story are traditions that keep her near.

**Teresa T.** We had the same dilemma at a family function in which we were missing my uncle whom we lost in March. I wrote a little something to read and we all had a bite of his favorite chocolate cake. It added a padding of memory to the punch of loss.

**Lee Ann S.** I lost my mother this past July. Every time we ate sweet stuff I thought of Momma, who would always say "bring me some leftovers and something sweet." I made a big batch of whisky balls . . .

**Beata N.** I treasure the many Christmas items that my mother gave to me over the years before dementia and death took her away. Many still carry the gift tags in her handwriting. Now, I am beginning to pass these treasures on to my children and grand-children a little at a time.

**Kimberly C.** "Building ON traditions." Not the same. A foundation to build different.

# JANUARY

## Beach Babies

January 14. A sunny crisp 43 degrees outside. There was no stopping her. She was so, so happy. My little land-living mermaid. And beside me sleeping as I type this, my sand shark.

---

*COMMENTS:*

**Cindy G-B.** You would think it was summertime!

**Judy Z.** Made me check my calendar!

**Taylor N.** A spirit that's free.

**Willis M.** A mermaid is a mermaid, no matter the temperature.

## MONTH THIRTY-NINE: Mutt Moves On

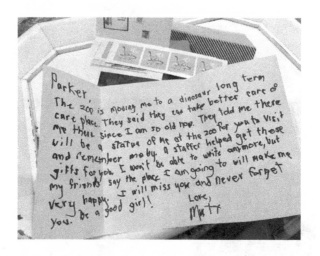

The letter was Fedexed. Parker hadn't heard from Mutt in a while, and the package was a welcome surprise.

You know the story: Years ago, Parker saw a realistic mechanical dinosaur exhibit and didn't know the plant-eating dino with a sweet smile and rounded teeth wasn't real. We named him Mutt. Parker talked about him to everyone, including her grandmother Zizi in Kentucky. Letters from Mutt started arriving in the mail; Parker never noticed they were postmarked Louisville.

Zizi never expected—none of us expected—for Parker to still believe almost three years later.

I didn't think too much about it when Parker said she was learning about dinosaurs in first grade, but Zizi got worried. What if she starts telling her friends about her pen pal? What if she tries to tell them dinosaurs are alive? What if she adamantly fights them—Parker's persistence is already legendary—and they make fun of her?

What if she starts blaming us for perpetuating a lie?

All great questions.

In typical grandmotherly fashion, Zizi came up with an answer. I knew she must have landed on one when a package arrived on our doorstep from Mutt. Parker read the handwritten note out loud with huge excitement.

*"Parker, the zoo is moving me to a dinosaur long-term care place."*

She looked up. I shrugged, equally curious.

*"They said they can take better care of me there since I am so old now. They told me there will be a statue of me at the zoo for you to visit and remember me by. A staffer helped get these gifts for you. I won't be able to write anymore, but my friends say the place I am going to will make me very happy. I will miss you and never forget you. Be a good girl! Love, Mutt"*

She stared at me.

"So Mutt won't write anymore?" Her voice had completely changed. She didn't wait for my answer. "What's a long-term care place?"

I tried to explain. I don't remember what I said, I only remember that she cut me off, to cut to the chase—

"Will he be happy?"

I pointed to the note. "The letter says he will be."

She looked down at the note again. "He said he'll miss me." She kissed the note. "I'll miss him too. I'm glad he'll be happy."

And then, somewhat surprisingly, that was that. Parker boxed the letter and stickers back up; they have been in her room ever since. Mutt moved on.

At some point, he had to, I know. Zizi did the brilliantly right thing, kindly saving her from some possible future foolishness (I can picture Parker standing up in class, debating whether ALL dinosaurs are dead). She'll be seven in a couple months, and it's pretty amazing she still believed Mutt was alive, sending her cards.

So why does it make me so sad?

---

*COMMENTS:*

**Cindy W.** We do all kinds of things to keep our babies from being hurt. That's our grandparent job.

**Christian V.** A brilliant close to the Mutt chapter!

**Ria M.** LOVE Zizi's beautiful ending to a magical friendship.

**Jody S.** One day she'll appreciate this whole story.

**Melissa P.** There are other magical things that kids "believe in" that must come to an end to save their feelings. Unfortunately, it seems to happen younger these days.

# FEBRUARY

## Monkey See, Monkey Do

Yesterday, Parker and I went to a fashion show where 100 percent of proceeds went to a children's hospital, and the patients acted as kid models. Parker has watched me emcee stuff her whole life: I had her at a motorcycle charity ride at only three weeks old. Only yesterday, when I got up on stage to kick things off . . . she followed. It wasn't planned for her to do so, but she did. And then once we were in front of 350 women, she kindly asked if she could help "talk about the outfits."

Laughter sprinkled throughout the room. How cute. She'd never done this before; I didn't know what to expect. But someone handed her her own microphone and she held it confidently, so after I read the first outfit description, I asked her what she thought.

She put that mic up close to her mouth and began to calmly chat with six-year-old commentary. No nerves. No fear. Great word choices in an easy-to-understand tone. I asked her after the second child model, and the third, and then the fourth . . . she never reused descriptive words, and became really funny with what she said.

"That pink dress is great with young girls or big girls because skirts are comfortable, just not good for playing on the playground. And the green around the bottom is really pretty!"

It got to the point where she was at such ease, I exited the stage. I was no longer needed.

Parker even did the raffle and the door prizes without me.

Blown away, I went to the back of the room and stared at my girl. Public speaking is a talent and I've never been so proud, so scared, and so very rattled by the in-charge kid voice coming through the speakers. Monkey see, monkey do, and I was a mom unnerved by her daughter's ability to absorb it all and play it back to me.

COMMENTS:

**Brian H.** She's had years of training! I took these at the CureSearch Walk in 2012. She never left your side, despite all the activity.

**Christine P.** I was there—she did a marvelous job and I was amazed at how articulate she was in calling out the raffle numbers, too. Like mother, like daughter.

**Sherry B.** First thing I noticed was how she was holding the mic in the second photo. She knows what to do.

**Alice A.** My daughters and I attended this event. We were amazed at Parker's words, tone, confidence, and poise.

**Debbie Mc.** They are what we sow.

**Steve M.** Why are you surprised? None of the rest of us are.

 **Molly:** Going over notes before the show.

## MONTH FORTY: Dance Mom

We're smiling. The weekend is over.

Parker has been really discouraged these past two days, which left me feeling protective and crazed. The two of us spent Saturday and Sunday at our first dance convention, for a total of seventeen hours. It was her first opportunity to experience a competitive level of contemporary, ballet, jazz, hip-hop, musical theater, tap, free-form . . . I don't even know what else. This is not my arena. I played other sports growing up and am confused by the TV reality shows following little girls and boys dressed up in costumes, learning intricate routines in half an hour. I can only say the classes I witnessed this weekend were a cross between "feel your body and let the music slowly move you," and half-step speedy moves that could be performed alongside Beyoncé.

It was only after the whole thing that I learned some of the teachers working with my daughter do actually tour with Brittany Spears and Rihanna.

I'll admit, from the corner of a cramped parent-viewing chair, stuck on the sideline of a convention center room for seventeen hours, I found myself mentally questioning one thing on repeat: *How did we get here?*

Parker loves her once-a-week dance classes as much as she loves soccer, school, and playing with neighborhood friends. She has never been a child focused on only one thing. But her dance school leader called a month ago and said she thought Parker was ready for the experience and invited her to this show. The other local girls in her studio who were invited dance three to four times a week and often perform together, but Parker seemed excited when I told her. We were in.

Fast-forward to yesterday. The kids in attendance were generally ages seven and up, so at only six, Parker was the youngest. Her height helped hide her age. She didn't appear to be behind everyone if you saw her talking with them; it was only obvious when the music started.

I had torn feelings watching her struggle. She knew she wasn't at the same level and kept hearing other girls' names and numbers pinned on their leotards called out with accolades. I watched her work 100 percent hard to only pick up 50 percent of the moves. Half the time she was doing it, and half the time she was three steps behind. Her personal frustration with herself was exceptionally hard to witness.

But here's what else I saw: tenacity.

My girl didn't give up.

My girl. Did not. Give up.

Near my cramped seat were a couple dozen other parents in their own chairs watching their own kids. All were moms of this "mini" group of dancers, ages six to nine. When you spend an entire weekend with women, you get to know them. You start to like them. You think you will be friends. You're in a bubble of a ballroom, thrown together because your girls have a similar love of dance.

During lunch, the bubble broke a bit. All ages poured out from their own classes in their own rooms and ate together in loosely formed hallway groups. Each dance company generally wants to sit with their own teammates. This meant I had a bird's-eye view to watch juniors and teens from Parker's dance facility—incredible dancers—warm up and talk about their morning classes. Their fake eyelashes and makeup were on point. Their bodies were flexible, their abs amazing. I kept looking from them to my daughter ten yards away, sitting picnic-style with a box lunch we'd ordered. Parker was laughing and trying to make friends, wearing Target leggings and a tank top that covered her stomach. These older girls wore lycra, sports bras, and sequins that somehow merged to create an athletic, sexiness.

Parker asked me exactly once about having a different outfit that looked more like what others were wearing. She didn't press it when I said she was already perfect and looked great. She also, God love her, patiently understood when I got called into the newsroom on Saturday. International televangelist Billy Graham had just died, and his body was being brought through Charlotte. He was headed to lie in repose at the library named in his honor. My bosses called—they wanted a weekday team to anchor the coverage, which meant I had to leave my strong-willed daughter with those other moms I'd just met . . . gracious women who acted like they understood having to suddenly work a breaking story.

It was hard leaving that convention center to head to the station. As much as I wasn't sure I belonged inside as a dance mom, it was difficult to walk out not holding my baby girl's hand. I questioned my priorities. But, you can't plan around headlines. This was a career I'd worked my life for, and when big news happens, it happens. All that said, leaving Parker alone yesterday for the last two hours with her water bottle, tap shoes, and other people did not feel good in my gut.

I told her Wes would pick her up, then got the moms' numbers to him, and his number to them. The other moms, I told Parker, would text him and he'd be there when she was done. I told her Wes couldn't wait to see her and was proud of her, just like I was. She didn't blink. She, in fact, gave me a big hug when I pulled her out of class to tell her all those things, then went right back into the dance group with no issues.

I proceeded on to the station. Threw on an extra dress I always leave there in case of unplanned situations like these, put on makeup, got debriefed on all facts, and anchored the cut-in as Billy Graham's body was brought through Charlotte. Then did the 6 p.m. and 11 p.m. shows after that. Got home past midnight and woke up again this morning to start round two of dance convention.

Parker was a bit reluctant to go this morning. She was dragging through eating her cereal. She didn't get mad at me when I read this morning's schedule wrong and got us there late, interrupting a ballet class and breaking etiquette rule number one. I think she was relieved to only have to do part of the class. In a later class, she got so lost in the fast-paced hip-hop impossible for virtually everyone, that she came in my lap to cry. I rubbed the back of her sweaty braid as her head was in my lap, but again, she got back up minutes after we wiped her tears and, with pushing, went back out for another three hours.

She never asked to go home.

She didn't wave the white flag.

She was a warrior. An overshadowed warrior.

I have never, ever been more proud of my hippie princess.

I'm staring out a window as I write this. We've been home an hour and Parker is in the yard, back in her element, running around with her neighborhood friends, playing imaginary games and ordering them around. They're screaming with laughter. Watching her skip and jump in a crowd where she feels comfortable, I'm left with too many thoughts about a weekend where we were both fish out of water. So often, we find our own tribes and stay in groups and places we know. We, as people, like ease. But this weekend, Parker and I branched out. We tried new things. She made friends at lunch, and I exchanged numbers with some great women, a few who have already texted. It was a radically different experience from how we normally spend weekends, and one—who knows?— we'll maybe try again sometime.

Either way, Miss Independent—who I see trying to ride a skateboard on grass right now in the backyard—rolled with the punches and proved adaptability and fortitude can be worth more than a blue ribbon.

---

*COMMENTS:*

**Darcy S.** I came back to reread this several times. All I can think of when reading this is my mom and I through my online college experience. She encouraged me, wiped my tears, and cheered me on when I accomplished something I thought I failed. She kept pushing me over and over again when I wanted to give up college and just find a job I wouldn't like. Because of her, I am graduating next year, a year and a half early. I love what you wrote about Parker's and your experience this weekend. The tears and not giving up. It's what I love about your relationship you have with Parker and what I love about mine with my mom. This touched my heart and soul in so many ways.

**Jessica W.** Our first-grade girl, K, is also a dancer, loves her friends fiercely, and is trying soccer (2nd time around) this week. Her style and independence along with the sass makes me want to scream most days, but also congratulate her individuality.

**Nora A.** I danced for 16 years and did those same long day conventions she did. It's not for the faint of heart and sounds like she took it like a pro. You learn so much at them, both in technique and mental stamina.

**Heather H.** I'm a Dance Mom—dance conventions are no joke. Trust me when I say even the experienced dancers struggle. It's tough stuff keeping up with back-up dancers to Taylor Swift and Beyoncé!

**Wyn W.** It's ironic to me because I was just looking for a quote from Rev. Billy Graham to share at work to kick off our Monday department huddle. His death last week has hit me hard. I was struck by this one: "Mountaintops are for views and inspiration, but fruit is grown in the valleys." You allowed Parker a valley and she showed you that she is capable of growth.

**Janet G.** I spent eight hours at a cheer competition myself on Saturday to watch my granddaughter's team compete with their 3-minute routine.

## Marker Face

Didn't hear them for twenty minutes. Turns out his sister was practicing her handwriting, using his face as her paper, and playing art class with a blond, shaggy canvas.

*COMMENTS:*

**Marcene H.** Looks like Hutch will let Parker do anything she wants.

**Patricia G.** My mom always said if they're quiet more than 5 minutes you'd better go see what they've done.

**Mike R.** Style points, Parker!

## HUH?

I agreed to teach Parker's first-grade class a couple of days from now for ninety minutes. Her teacher just emailed to ask about a lesson plan. No problem thinking of fifty-eight headlines for newscasts today, but I have zero ideas on what to bring to a class full of six-year-olds.

## Teaching Oz

Last night, I asked Parker what she'd like her class to learn while I filled in. Her most excellent teacher was going to a special awards lunch, and when an email went around asking for volunteers, I eagerly signed up. Early afternoon was a rare time for her class to need help: this felt like it had my name all over it.

Parker said her whole school is learning about countries, and her class is supposed to present on Australia for Multicultural Night, a big open house the school puts on next month. *Perfect*, I thought. During college I lived outside Sydney for six months doing a study-abroad program. Clearly this would be a breeze.

So today, I took in pictures, a lesson plan, and then . . . after teaching for twenty minutes . . . I had nothing left. The kids were distracted. First graders have a low threshold for boredom. It also turns out ninety minutes is an eternity. I ended up tying shoes, fixing Band-Aids, letting everyone take too many potty breaks, heading off a thousand tattletales, and making this class full of breathing jumping beans fall into any activity I could find.

Teaching is the toughest profession out there. Bar none. I bow down to every elementary school leader in the world. Thank you, Ms. K., for letting me borrow your class.

Thank you even more for taking them back.

---

*COMMENTS:*

**Caron W.** So many times, we teachers say something like "I wish the outside world could see what it is we actually do in a day." The kids probably learned more than you believe! P.S. I teach kindergarten.

**Liz B.** Many people have opinions about what teachers should do (especially those who make decisions for us), however very few darken the door of a school or classroom to volunteer.

**Diana S.** When my kids were in elementary school, I would spend an hour in the classroom every week, helping with whatever the teacher needed. After that hour, I was ready to go home! I could never do what teachers do .

**Andrea O.** I've taught for 13 years. It's hard, but incredibly worthwhile. Sincerely, A Tired First Grade Teacher.

**Nancy W.** As a retired Charlotte-Mecklenburg Schools principal, I wish more people would volunteer for a couple hours just to see how hard our teachers do work. The unsung heroes of our city.

**Albert P.** My fiancée is a pre-k teacher. She has the patience of Job.

**Julie C.** One class party or field trip, and I need a break.

**Brenda B.** I was a first grade teacher, and eventually burned out. We were expected to be social workers, psychologists, therapists, police, magicians, and also teach.

## MONTH FORTY-ONE: Half Angel, Half Devil

My sweet little cherub nugget has stubborn, crafty, devilish blood running through his tiny veins. He is an adorable force to be reckoned with, a spritely little charmer who sucks you in and then turns against you. He'll start a sentence with, "I love you, Mommy..." and end it with, "... you're stupid."

Except because he's three, it comes out sounding like:

"I wuv you, Mawmmy . . . yurr stoopid."

Then he'll laugh maniacally, not even aware of what he's saying, but knowing he shouldn't say it. It's a big, open-mouth cackle, showing all twenty baby teeth.

To yell at him makes him laugh. To tell him not to say something makes him say it even louder. To ignore him makes him say it on repeat. And to put him in a time out is futile . . . he just sings loudly while staring at the wall, alone, happy, totally unbothered that he's being punished. He's impossible.

Also, when he decides something—he's done. That's it. You can't change his mind. You are either with him or you're wrong. Hutch will be a great negotiator later in life, because he doesn't actually budge a smidge on whatever he thinks, so people just give in.

Which is why drawing a line with him is necessary. I had to do it last weekend, which is the second picture in the split-screen collage. A mile into a leisurely walk down a neighborhood greenway, we needed to turn around. He refused. He wanted to walk farther. He said no a few times . . . then simply stopped. Rather than escalating into screams, he sat and settled into a silent but strong pouting protest.

I ultimately walked away and left him. Went far enough back up the walkway where he couldn't see me behind the trees but I could see him . . . and waited TWENTY MINUTES until he finally screamed my name with shrill fear, thinking he'd been abandoned in the cold. Cruel parenting? Maybe. But when he's in mini-terrorist mode, you have to stay a creative step ahead.

There's no ordering Hutch, no convincing him, no bribing him. He's a towheaded brick wall who half the time is—by choice—not even listening.

Unless you bring up work passes. Or keys. Or food. Then he's 1000 percent focused and hanging on your every word.

On the flip side, he's the most loving boy in the world. Parker had an independent streak a mile wide from an early age. Hutch clings more. He needs me. He asks to be held. He rushes into my hugs.

He tackles my legs every time I come home on a dinner break and is always the first to greet me, tug at my arms, and ask for "more kisses" before I leave again.

He'll also ask about my day—actually say out loud, "Tell me your day, Mommy" (sounds like: "Tellll me yurr day, Mawmmy"), because he's heard me say it a thousand times to him, his sister, and Wes when I walk in the door. Again, he may not really be aware of what he's saying, but he says it because it elicits a reaction. Though in this case, a loving one. I always hug him a second time after he asks.

One child, two extremes.

Angel and devil.

Also commonly referred to as the terrible threes.

---

*COMMENTS:*

**Amy B.** Love the quilt he is snuggled in! Reminds me of family heirlooms my grandma made years ago.

 **Molly.** We had it made from some of my mom's special old clothes. Each piece is a fabric she wore. We call it "Grammy's blanket." Hutch loves it (that's his angel side).

**Leigh L.** Terrible two's—no!! Terrible three's—absolutely.

**Jenny A.** Also known as threenagers.

**Margaret B.** I had a challenging Hutch and he is now 23 and still the sweetest "little boy" that loves his Mama.

**Philip C.** I have a 22-year-old that was, and is that way. He did become a great negotiator.

**Karen D.** My beautiful hard-headed son questioned everything. Wanted his way. Made up his mind and never budged. But loved his momma. He is now 29, and a captain in the army.

**Pamela G.** I have a negotiator as well. Instead of picking option A or B, she comes up with option C and proceeds to convince you why her option is better.

**Christian B.** I literally am at a loss for words looking at the two pictures. They're perfect.

# APRIL

## MONTH FORTY-TWO: Bionic Eyes

It's funny how things start. Years ago I was telling Parker about manners, and I said it was important to try to make her parents proud. From there, I lied. Casually. Said even if I wasn't in the room with her, I could still always see what she was doing.

She was probably three years old at the time and didn't let me get away with such a foolish statement.

"How can you always see what I'm doing, Mommy?"

"Because I have bionic eyes, honey."

That reply popped in my head, and I said it. No idea why. She looked confused, of course. Preschoolers don't know the word bionic.

"What are bee-awn-ic eyes?"

"Bionic eyes. Like, um, a special power. Even when I'm not around you I can always see you."

She then proceeded to ask two dozen questions. Did "bee-awn-ic" mean I could see her if my back was turned? Could I see her if she was outside and I was inside? Could I also hear her voice, or did my special power only witness actions? Parker kept asking, and I kept tap dancing out explanations. All kinds of rules and parameters were set in that moment, her insatiable curiosity forcing me to double down on the concept and (quickly) dream up details to convince her I'd always see how she was acting.

By the end, I was almost convinced as well.

That little fib turned into a wickedly fantastic parenting tool.

For four years—up until last weekend—Parker believed I had bionic eyes. I used them as a creative way to keep her in check. She'd be at a friend's house playing and when I'd pick her up, the other girl's mom would tell me what they did. Later that night I'd say to Parker, "How was catching fireflies with Julia?" or "Did you like the ice cream you had with Lizzie?"

She'd act surprised I knew. I'd just smile and say, "Bionic eyes."

The fact she thought I was always watching kept her a little more honest. Which was ironic, as I was full-on lying. But you don't mess with what works. I've even heard her explain to Hutch from a different room, "No, Hutchie, don't do that. Mommy's bee-awn-ic eyes will see you."

Finally, last Saturday—her seventh birthday—the gig was up.

I knew she'd eventually be mature enough to realize it was all fictitious, and I wanted to end it before she figured it out on her own. So six months ago, I told her when she turned seven, my bionic eyes expired. They'd still work for Hutch, but a parent's supersight wanes when a child enters true "big kid" stage. They have to be more responsible for themselves, even when Mommy isn't watching.

In typical Parker fashion, she absorbed every word and never forgot. This past Saturday, she woke up thrilled about her birthday, came downstairs to see the traditional balloons, streamers, and three gifts, and looked right at me with the largest smile on her seven-year-old face.

"Mommy, today I turn seven! Your bee-awn-ic eyes are gone!"

That's the first thing she said.

I almost felt guilty. My insides felt like they were receiving an actual kick. She had felt policed more than necessary, more than I maybe realized, for years.

But on the other hand, she's a really great kid who is smart and kind to others and generally does the right thing.

So maybe it worked?

Either way, those bionic eyes are now gone.

I hope decades from now Parker will get a good laugh out of this when she's trying to corral her own little ones (as opposed to wanting to kill me). Maybe she'll tell them she can always see them... through walls, in different cities, and definitely when they're about to be rotten and think no one is watching.

The best stories are the ones never planned.

*COMMENTS:*

**Scott W.** In our family all the parents have eyes in the back of their heads. They're kinda magic because even if you comb through my wife's hair looking for them, kids can't see them.

**Lisa S.** Molly, what you can tell her now is that moms and dads do have friends everywhere and she may never know who sees her and reports on the good or bad behavior. "Remember, I have spies everywhere."

**Teresa C.** For years, my mom had my two boys convinced that she was 21. Then one day my oldest son realized the math didn't work out. We still laugh about it.

**Marjorie G.** Hmmm . . . where were your bee-awn-ic eyes when Parker used permanent markers on Hutch's face and hair?

 **Molly.** She literally asked the same thing when I found Hutch covered in marker. I think because I hadn't come running immediately—she assumed I was watching—it was okay to keep coloring him. I told her I'd turned them off temporarily. She bought it. Another example of why I knew I had to wrap this little lie up.

**Stephen P.** Elf on the Shelf called. He's not happy you're trying to cut him out of a job.

**Terrance T.** Oh, what a tangled web we weave . . .

# MAY

## Scrubs

Dr. Hutch wore his new scrubs and badge to preschool. I let him.
He might be half devil, but he sure can charm the heck out of me.

---

*COMMENTS:*

**Doug H.** Don't blink.

**Gianna L.** Sometimes with my children I get a glimpse of how they
will look when they are fully grown. It's scary and wonderful all at
the same time.

## Recital

This picture has been on my phone, staring me in the face since Saturday. Her dance recital was a success, but the point is the undeniable, unavoidable, unacceptable truth this photo screams every single second I see it:

I turned around, and missed my little girl.

*COMMENTS:*

**Geri E.** She is spunky.

She is sassy.

She is simple.

She is complicated.

She is unique.

She is you.

She is innocent.

She is wise.

She is beautiful.

She is kind.

She is a force to be unleashed.

She is her mother's daughter through and through.

Though she looks old, she's still your little girl.


**Elizabeth Y.** Just wait. It happens faster and faster. Somehow I'm signing my sweet boy up for middle school football and planning a 5th grade moving up ceremony. Ten minutes ago he was obsessed with Thomas the Train and Toy Story.

## MONTH FORTY-THREE: Magic Earmuffs

Parker gave me the most beautifully insightful Mother's Day gift last weekend. She got them out of our winter clothes Christmas basket and wrapped them in a birthday gift bag. She woke me up out of bed, excited. Couldn't wait for me to open them.

"Earmuffs?" I asked, confused.

"Magic mommy earmuffs!" she replied. "You put them on when I whine and Hutch calls people stupid. If you wear them, you won't hear us anymore."

Oh. My.

She. Is. Genius.

Hutch had since wandered in and turned on my TV, so I immediately got back in bed and wore the gift to block out *Peppa Pig*. They also worked for *Jessie*, a Disney Channel show I think teaches too many junior-high-level things, and lasted through *Ben & Holly's Little Kingdom*, a British cartoon Hutch loves that I can't stand.

There I was, lying down with earmuffs, as they happily watched too much TV. (Parker took this picture of us in that moment.)

Hours later, we were in the driveway. Wes had asked what I wanted for Mother's Day, and I had one small, sole request: my favorite store had 20 percent off everything, and I wanted to go there before attempting a family dinner. Wes said if that's what I wanted, we'd of course all go. Family-style.

But Parker wasn't on board. Her morning kindness had evaporated, and she wanted to play with friends. She stood outside the car whining, relaying all the reasons *she* shouldn't have to go to *my* favorite store. About this time, Hutch decided he no longer needed a car seat and death-gripped the front dashboard so he wouldn't have to move into the back. It was an ugly chorus of head-ringing proportions.

Then I remembered: earmuffs.

I went back inside. They were in my hands when I returned. Parker sighed. Huh? She stopped fussing long enough to sigh? It surprised me even more when she then—on her own—got into the car. Hutch carried on with his antics, until I put on the earmuffs. It took a good minute, but he stopped the tantrum to test me: "Mommy? Mommy?? MOMMY??!?!"

I pretended I couldn't hear him. I said as if I didn't know he was around, "I will only hear you when I take these off. I will only take these off when you get in your car seat."

He let go of the dashboard and moved toward the back.

I was floored.

I removed them in the car. But five miles into our drive, just for fun, just to get under his skin, Parker took Hutch's new coloring book and bragged she'd color all his pages first, intentionally aggravating him because she could. He immediately tried to tattle, and I turned and threatened them both that if they didn't figure it out, I'd return to Earmuff World, a place where their voices made no impact.

She kept it up. He yelled. I put them on and bumbled down I-77 in 94-degree weather, wearing winter earmuffs. She noticed. Turning to Hutch, she returned his coloring book.

He said, "Thank you, my seester."

She replied, "You're welcome."

THESE *WERE* MAGIC.

We got to the mall, and I put the earmuffs in my purse.

My favorite store was slammed. Wes, Hutch, and Parker dutifully tagged along. The kids were behaving, and Wes, like many men in the store on this particular day, quietly hung near the front. The kids didn't want to stay with him, and I understood why. The front was boring; the store was exciting. Blinded by the pretty clothes and sale prices, I forgot what terrors they could be and said they could come with me to look. Ten minutes later, I got cocky. I thought, "Surely they will behave themselves a little longer," and grabbed a mess of clothes to try on.

When near the front of the dressing room line madness, the kind lady looked at us and said they only had one oversized room open. But there was a time limit on it, she explained. They were just so crowded. "No problem," I replied. "The kids will be fine. It won't take long."

Once in that room and halfway into dress number two with six more to go—and for absolutely no reason—Hutch did a running tackle on Parker in the six-by-six-foot space. She let out a wail more from surprise than pain, then smacked him back. He dropped dramatically and pretended to cry. I picked him up and moved him on the other side of me, away from her, but still all of us within arms' distance.

I firmly told them to get it together.

He stepped toward her. I glared.

"I wahhnna tell my seester sawry."

I nodded. He approached with outstretched apologetic arms . . . and they fell to the ground in a laughing, loud, hug. As they dropped, the door handle was somehow hit and opened on us, me half-dressed, flashing anyone who could see. I slammed it shut. The noise was explosive. Hutch stood up with excitement. "I wahhnna do it! My turn! I shuuut da door!"

This was not a game, I told him. The door must stay shut.

"NOOOOOooooo . . . I shuuut da door!"

He grabbed at it and ripped it open, and suddenly the three of us were staring at the lovely mass of people—some men forced from the front of the store to wait for their wives and mothers in a lobby-like spot of the dressing room that had chairs.

"SHUT IT NOW." I was loud and clenched teeth combined.

He slammed it so hard all four walls shook.

"I do zit ahgain!"

"NO, HUTCH." I said. "NO ONE DOES THAT AGAIN."

He started to cry. Shoulders down.

"Mom," Parker cut in. She looked like a babysitter looks when the child they're temporarily caring for is being a brat.

"WHAT?" I was mortifyingly mad and embarrassed. I just wanted to try on the remaining clothes and didn't know why three-year-old Hutch couldn't just *sit* there, when really I knew it was my fault for having him in this terribly confined space. And honestly, why can't dressing rooms be big enough for dumb moms who take kids with them on Mother's Day?

"Why don't you just wear your earmuffs?" Parker said. "Then you can't hear him grab the door."

"Because he can't open the door, Parker," I said with a harsher tone than she deserved. "Blocking his noise is good, but he can't open the door when I'm trying on clothes." I was certain people in the waiting room could hear.

"I can stand with my back on the door. I'm stronger than him."

My girl. She was trying. She could sense my frustration and was trying, Plus, her idea was the only one available.

"Can you make sure you he doesn't open it?"

"Yes," she said.

"Are you positive?" I couldn't think of another option besides just leaving.

"Yes," she said. "But you better wear the earmuffs so he knows you can't hear him if he yells."

So that's what we did. He stopped crying when he saw me pull the earmuffs out of my purse. He tried to open and shut that wooden dressing room door, while Parker put her mental strength into keeping him hopeful it'd open, and her physical strength into stretching her arms wide, her legs apart and positioning her body to look like a defensive lineman. Her mission, which she was choosing to accept, was to keep that door closed.

And, me? I tried on summer clothes wearing winter woolen pink earmuffs. It worked. Got through the whole potential pile.

There is no picture of all that, of course. There was no time for some selfie. But I do have one from when they were wrestling on the cement floor.

Mother's Day. I have yet to experience one where it's pretty pictures and a beautiful brunch, but I have plenty that create rewarding stories for our scrapbook of life.

Also, if you see me walking around in public wearing earmuffs as I tug two kids along, don't judge.

*COMMENTS:*

**Susan W.** I feel your pain but can't quit laughing.

**MaryLou W.** These stories take me back to a time when my two older children were trying on bathing suits at Belk, all while the 3-year-old was behind me taking off her clothes. As I turned around, she threw back the curtain and proceeded to run a 100-dash down the center aisle stark naked.

**Sharon W.** This is genius! You do realize that half the Charlotte moms will be sporting winter earmuffs in June!

**Amanda D.** Thank you. Thank you. Thank you. Now I know my kids are halfway normal.

**Lesa A.** Proof that Hutch only whines because you listen.

**Sharon W.** Can you *really* be sure there are no other pics? LOL.

# JUNE

## Last Day

She just graduated first grade. He couldn't be more proud.

---

*COMMENTS:*

**Della B.** You can see the love on Parker's face for Hutch.

**Thom B.** Congrats, Parker. Hutch is obviously crazy about you.

**Wayne K.** I think it's the kids that rule us.

## MONTH FORTY-FOUR: Surfer Girls

She looked at me from her prone position, gripping the rails. She didn't call my name—I already knew she wouldn't do that out of not wanting to appear scared—but her eyes told the story. She was not comfortable. It's not often that Parker is not comfortable.

From my board where I waited for my own wave, floating parallel to the shore on purpose so she could see me, I returned her look.

"It's okay, P."

She didn't reply.

Mason, the sunburned fifteen-year-old assigned to her, suddenly said, "Here we go. Start paddling, Parker!"

He gave her a push into a foot-tall small hill of water, and her arms rotated on either side of the board.

"Push up now!" Mason said loudly.

My seven-year-old locked her arms out straight, as if she was about to do a push-up, then lunged her left leg forward while keeping her right leg back—yes, that's it! Then she fell.

She couldn't stand in the water but quickly bubbled up to the top. Mason was there.

"Almost, Parker. You almost got up." He helped her back on the board and paddled her back out to where I was still leisurely floating. It was low tide.

I learned to surf many years ago when studying abroad in Australia. I was never good, but always enjoyed it and went out in low tides. When Parker mentioned she wanted a lesson, I figured we should do it together. Retrain myself.

But now my thoughts weren't on if I could do it again; they were on my girl.

Though she remained silent, my trained mom eye saw her gripping the rails even harder, with her mouth set firmly straight. She was anxious. I could also tell that Mason, a super-blond, longer-haired guy with a teenage-boy smile, looking the exact adorable part of a young, laid-back North Carolina surfer, wasn't reading these quiet distress signs from a seven-year-old girl.

He'd been kind and cool, getting her to talk as they walked down the beach, him carrying her board, asking her about her favorite movies. But now they were in the water, and she was fully dependent on his voice and an eight-foot beginner board with rubber fins. I was in sight, but not within reach. It was too much for her. I knew it was. But unless she broke into tears, he wasn't going to notice.

As I debated whether to say something and sound like a protective mother, a voice from a board to our right broke into my head.

"Hey, Mason," it said. "Take her in closer. Ride the white waves. Take her up there first."

It was Tony, a professional surfer and owner of this surf school. Tony is a celebrity in Carolina Beach, which is next to Kure. Brochures show him on huge waves and his name, Tony Silvagni, covers flyers. Hours ago, when we first approached the surf-school tiki hut—stationed in a dingy but well-located parking lot near the sand, a vibe of how true beach businesses operate—we heard all about how Tony was born and raised here, but now travels the world competing and comes back in summers to run surf lessons in his hometown.

And here he was, saving me from having to save my little girl. He saw Parker's death grip on her board from twenty yards away.

"Sure, man."

Mason looked at Parker and said something, and they moved in, farther away from me.

Minutes later, Tony, Mason, my own surf instructor, Lennie, and a handful of others bobbing out in the ocean all saw Parker catch the whitewater from a wave that had already broken, push up on the board by herself, lunge her feet into position, stand up straight, and ride that board the whole way to shore.

"That's it!" Tony yelled. I'm sure she couldn't hear, but it didn't matter. We all knew she felt good about herself when she jumped off into ankle-deep water with her fist pumped in the air. Lennie laughed.

"She's a spitfire, huh?" I looked at him. Lennie was closer to my age, with more maturity about him.

"Always," I said.

"Your turn," he said. I could taste the salt on my lips from where water had splashed up. "Wave's here. Go."

I started paddling. I could hear Lennie behind me, "Now!"

I popped up and stood . . . for about two seconds. My fall was accompanied with an unattractive splash. Being a competitive swimmer all through my childhood and high school, I knew how to recover, but also knew how awkward I must have appeared.

When I got back on the board, I looked ahead. Parker was riding her second wave, arms outstretched this time, knees slightly bent, looking legit. It was as if my mermaid-hippie-princess had been doing this her whole life.

After trying out a few more waves, I stayed on. Lennie was the perfect teacher, telling me how surfing is a little like riding a bike: your mind has memory of the technique; your body just feels different twenty years later. "You have to remind yourself of the feel," he said. "Pop up and grip with your feet, balance with your body, and control the board while also being controlled by the wave."

 C3&O

An hour later, Parker had ridden dozens of waves to shore, stopping to acknowledge Hutch, who was sitting there waiting patiently with Wes for the lesson to be done. She clearly felt like Queen of the Shallow End White Waves—I could feel her mojo across the water. I'd fallen as many times as I had stood, and considered it all a success.

As we were exiting the water, Hutch, in his swimmies, splashed toward us.

"Mama! Mama! Mama!"

Parker was holding my hand up in the champion pose you'd expect from a newly crowned ocean queen. I was reaching for Hutch.

"I wanna be surf someday," he said.

I wasn't sure I heard him right. The ocean was loud and Parker was distracting. "What, Hutch?"

"I wanna be surf someday. When I'm a big boy! I wanna be surf someday too!"

His white hair was half-invisible because it's so blond. His tan little face was looking up at me, and he had white zinc on his nose because he burns easily. His blue shirt matched the rash guards the instructors were wearing, and I'd borrowed one as well. He can't swim well yet but was wholly unafraid, running out to meet his girls in the waist-high ocean.

I smiled at him.

Mason came over, dragging her board out and waving good-bye. "Thanks, Parker. You were awesome."

I looked at Mason, then looked back at Hutch. Then looked back at Mason.

The only difference was twelve years.

⊂੪੭

How easy to forget that kids learn what they see and want what they watch. Hutch sat in the sand for an hour, absorbing from shore. The paid lesson was for Parker, but the longer-lasting education is what Hutch—with his overgrown haircut, his whatever attitude and love of water—drank in: a view of his girls standing on waves, falling in, and getting back up to start over.

No one has a crystal ball, but as I watched Mason walk up the beach and heard Parker tell Hutch it was "Awesome!" I couldn't help but think surfboards were a sure part of my little boy's future.

---

*COMMENTS:*

**William A.** Tony is a pillar in the Carolina/ Kure Beach communities. My own long blond-haired surfer started in his camp.

**June P.** Kure and Carolina are a gift to many.

**Joe W.** Feel like I've just been to the beach.

**Coffey W.** I can smell the salt air.

**Susan H.** I remember my very first trip to Crescent Beach, SC. My family was an average American family making a living working 40-hour weeks in textiles. The July 4th shutdown provided everyone a much-needed vacation.

**Kinzie D.** What a rush!

 **Molly.** Before. Mentally owning it.

## The Guide in GPS

This sign is in Smithfield, Johnston County, southeast of Raleigh, on the street where my dad and his sisters grew up. Where every Thanksgiving was spent in my grandparents' house, where the wide screened-in porch housed rocking chairs, sweet tea, and the smell of my Pop-Pop's tobacco pipe.

I haven't been back to Smithfield for a long time. There was no real reason to go: most everyone has passed or moved on. Though it's a piece of me, it doesn't call me to return.

Driving to Kure Beach for this vacation, we went through Raleigh to visit my youngest brother, Stewart. Kure is a straight shot down I-40 East. Leaving Raleigh, I checked the GPS for directions. I don't know why. It's a simple route, one I know well, but something drew me to map it.

The phone told me to leave the interstate and get on Highway 70. Via Smithfield.

I checked again. Same directions. Go through Smithfield. There must be a wreck, I thought. We got off I-40 East and on Highway 70.

GPS took us through downtown Smithfield. Past the McDonald's where Pop-Pop got daily morning coffee with his other grandfather friends. They all met early every weekday, and it seemed like he never missed it. If grandkids were visiting, he'd possibly take us with him. I have a distinct memory of him asking me to read to his friends, to show off that his granddaughter liked books. My other cousin told me he once asked her to sing. Proud men, proud Pop-Pops, not wanting to brag with stories and words the way so many women do... instead saying little and showing their pride in action.

My memory banks were being stirred as the McDonald's appeared, then went in the rearview. I hadn't seen those particular arches for a long, long time.

The GPS then took us past the church where we had Pop-Pop's and Nana Lolly's funerals. It's a notable blue dome on the Main Street. I pointed out the church. Parker hasn't heard much about my dad's parents. She soaked it in. Hutch was clueless.

The McDonald's and pretty church are on relatively larger roads in Smithfield, so it didn't strike me as odd that GPS took us by such sentimental spots.

But it then told us to take a right on Third Street, into a neighborhood off the traveled thoroughfares.

"This is where Nana Lolly and Pop-Pop lived." I breathed the words out loud.

GPS took us straight down Third. Moments later, mouth open, I pointed.

"Parker," I said. "Look. It's East Parker Street."

She giggled from the backseat because her name was on a sign. But it wasn't funny. It was fate. I took this picture out of disbelief.

East Parker Street. Here we were on East Parker Street. I knew as I stared at this sign that the brick split-level with the screened-in porch was one block over on the corner of Second Avenue. I know my grandparents' old mailing address and zip code by heart, because my father used to make me write weekly letters to them starting in second or third grade. I hadn't thought of them or Smithfield or my dad's past—my past—in a long time, and yet here we were, with the GPS taking us straight to it.

We took a right onto Parker Street and I pointed out the house and the porch and told stories of how my dad, the grandfather Parker and Hutch never had a chance to know, loved coming home to Smithfield. I told them things he'd told me about his own childhood in this house, now in front of our eyes. I told them about my cousins and me playing in the wide driveway, and the smell of the pipe, and the basketball net that had once been there. I told them about Thanksgivings and the food displayed on lace doilies, and the attic upstairs, filled with boxes and cobwebs and every piece of junk my grandmother had never thrown away, and how us eleven grandchildren always considered it a treasure hunt to see what we could find. I spent lots of time talking about the Grantham Rummy Tournament, and how my dad taught me to play when I was Parker's age, and how we'd all bet on the cards, using pennies and nickels.

Parker laughed at that one.

"Did you name me after your daddy's house?"

I didn't expect her question. No, we didn't name Parker after East Parker Street. Not one bit. In fact, Wes chose her name after she was born. We'd been deciding between a couple, and he made the call right then and there in the hospital room. Until today, it had never even crossed my mind that the address I'd handwritten on an envelope every week for years and years was the same name we'd given our first child.

"No, honey," I said. "We didn't."

But what a beautiful detour and thought to have.

GPS soon spit us back on I-40 East. I never did check to see if there was a wreck on the interstate. I know it wasn't GPS that took us there.

❦

Two days after Father's Day, a rewarding holiday in many ways for many deserving people, and so hard for many others, I can finally write about this road trip to Kure. No doubt the force that took us through Smithfield wanted us to remember him, too. He wanted to show his grandchildren some of their history—his history— that I hadn't ever relayed.

A father is a father forever. Whether gone too young or holding your hand until he's 100. Sometimes they guide in person . . . sometimes in ways that can't be explained.

---

*COMMENTS:*

**Libby P.** My late uncle used to meet at that Smithfield McDonald's every morning for coffee with his old friends. They called the area where they sat "The Amen Corner."

**Penny C.** Lucky kids have dads who find ways to show up, and show pride.

**Linda M.** To have your way with words! You just took everyone who is from a simpler time down memory lane to all of our childhoods.

**Vicki S.** I lived in Carrboro during my UNC days. Years later I drove back through only to notice the street names in my complex. Abbey Lane and Cole Drive. Yep, my kids are Abbey and Cole. Carolina goes with you!

**Trina C.** When I saw the sign I thought you had named your daughter after it, too. Sometimes when I go through Lancaster, SC, I will ride by my grandparents' old house to experience the same kind of memories and feel them flooding back.

**Deborah W.** I have chills.

# JULY

## MONTH FORTY-FIVE: Captain America

Hutch and his bike helmet. Out to eat, sometimes in the car, hanging in the playroom, just watching TV. This would probably be of zero significance to most parents, but it makes me wonder.

Anyone who knows Hutch knows he used to wear a cranial band. He started at four months old, for twenty three hours a day. We had it painted electric green with the words *The Incredible Hutch* and a little cartoon Hulk-like baby. Months later, therapists recommended a second one because his head was still misshapen. We painted it the exact same, with *The Incredible Hutch II*. It didn't come off until his first birthday.

Those two helmets are now bookends in his room. (You can also see one on the cover of the first book.) They're stinking adorable, and I'll never get rid of them.

All that to say, no one forgets how Hutch was FORCED to wear a helmet for eight months straight.

Which is why it's perplexing that he now CHOOSES to wear one walking around in life.

It's not constant. Not every minute (like work badges around his neck), but Hutch often wakes up and plonks on his Captain America bike helmet, then asks me to help hook it under his chin. He'll come to me in the morning after dressing himself, wearing shoes, underwear, and this helmet. Nothing else. I start the day laughing.

He'll also wear it in public. We were on my dinner break when this picture was taken. He was freshly bathed, in pajamas, and insisted on wearing his helmet to meet Mommy out for a hot dog.

It's a harmless obsession, kinda like the work badges. Right? I think? Both make me laugh.

But unlike the work badges, this helmet thing also has me questioning childhood development and our subconscious psyches. Is there something in him that clings to the Incredible Hutch era? He wore that helmet during a formative time. He learned to eat and walk, and cut teeth in those eight months. Is there something about having his head protected and an added weight on all sides of his skull that makes him feel more comfortable?

Even if I never have an answer, I've learned over the previous forty-four months that if I have a thought about their growth, even a seemingly inane one, I need to write it down. You never know how it might fit into something later.

So, that's Month Forty-Five. Not mind-shattering brilliance . . . just a little brain-protecting.

---

*COMMENTS:*

**Jared S.** My baby had a cranial band too and now he hates hats—he won't put anything on his head.

**Abbey F.** I have twin boys. One wore a band as a baby and the other did not. The one that wore the band would keep hats on when he was a toddler, and the other one would rip them off. I had never thought of a correlation between the band/hat thing before.

**Jennifer E.** My son wore a cranial band for a year. A year or so later he went through a fedora phase. All fedoras. All the time. His favorite belonged to his great-great grandfather. Hiking? Fedora. School? Fedora (until they said no). Mall, dinner, movies, etc. Always wearing a fedora. Then one day, he stopped. I never made the connection between forced headwear and voluntary.

**Nina T.** [preschool teacher] I can't help but wonder if there is some feeling of security in the helmet. He is always going for head-wearing particular items when it's playtime in preschool, too…

## FaceTime

Parker and I just got off our nightly call. I often say good night from the newsroom, and she from her bedroom pillow. It's like she already knows that I do that call because it's the only way to see her and Hutch right before bedtime . . . as if she's already aware of the life lesson "you just do what you have to do" to show love.

---

*COMMENTS:*

**Darlene R.** I worked second and third shift all my working life. My kids knew it as normal. But they also knew I would get vacation days just for them—the "important days," they called them. I find it's harder on the parents sometimes than the kids themselves.

**Robert G.** It's all in perspective. Getting it done but not forgetting the little things.

# AUGUST

## Jellyfish

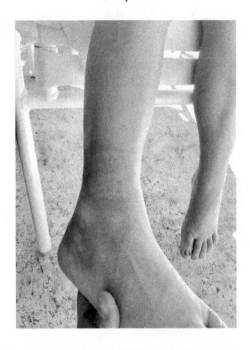

A jellyfish got in Parker's way. We're now listing what we'll do to this jellyfish if we ever get our hands on it. Parker suggested I use my work high heels to pin it to the wall. She wants Brown Bear to become real and eat it for lunch. Hutch had no good suggestions but asked if the jellyfish was gone . . . could he have its ocean pass?

*COMMENTS:*

**Ashley M.** We always take a spray bottle with us when we head to the ocean. It's ¾ white vinegar and ¼ water. When they get stung, spray it on the area and it takes the burn away super-fast! The lifeguard told us this years ago and we've done it ever since.

**Tiffany S.** I'm not trying to sound gross . . . I've heard if you let a little boy pee on the sting it helps the burn. Has anyone ever heard this? Bless her heart! Maybe someone should go find Hutch?

**John C.** I'm not laughing at what happened. I'm laughing at the creativity of her vengeful remedies.

**AngelaandTerry B.** Tell her it's dead now and we have a picture of it.

## MONTH FORTY-SIX: Summer Games

I ce cream.

M ostly at the pier.
I nstantly good.
S elect the flavor . . . then
S troll outside. See what fisherman caught.

K ites.
U nique old motels.
R ough boardwalk planks.
E ndless walks on sand.

B ritts.
E very morning.
A nd sometimes night.
C arefree afternoons.
H ang Ten Grill.

M usic.
U mbrellas.
S unkissed rays.
T anning without trying.

G o farther! Go farther!
O ver or under the waves?

B ook in beachbag.
A ctual reading, not done.
C ontentment.
K ismet contentment.

S and in your toes.
U ndercurrents swirling.
M ounds of towels.
M oms closely watching.
E verlasting view.
R ays absorbed.

A nother drink please?
L ying around.
M otivation nonexistent.
O kay with nothing all day.
S ee?
T aking it easy can be done.

O ftentimes throughout the year,
V ividly and
E ternally,
R emembering these sunny moments.

Summer is a gift, the beach its big red bow. Another season is all but wrapped.

*COMMENTS:*

**Shell M.** We're on a last minute family vacation in Hilton Head because I'm truly in denial that school starts next week. I took your book in my beach bag with good intentions, but sat in the waves with my kiddos for so long, that I didn't read any further. Whoops! Yet, I think you'd be proud.

**Audria H.** She looks just like you!

**Camille M.** Well said.

**Cybil W.** Your spitting image.

**Marsha K.** Speaking from someone who understands, the beach is in your soul.

**Chris L.** Love that chick.

**Bob B.** Getting into poetry now?

**Robby T.** I see what you did there.

## Uber

His own personal Uber. Every day he asks. Every day she picks up and delivers.

---

*COMMENTS:*

**Melissa L.** One day he will be bigger and provide the transportation. My big boy is still managing his brother but not for much longer. Comes in handy when you're trying to catch a shirt!

**Linda C.** I look at the closeness between these two and it reminds me so much of the bond I had like that with my younger brother. I lost him on 9/11/01 at the age of 45 (from a brain infection, not WTC). I've never been able to get over it.

**Rocky W.** Tip her well.

## Day One of Second Grade

COMMENTS:

**Milly G.** I still remember years ago when Parker started a week too early.

**Marty M.** And what's hanging around Hutch's neck?

**Sandra M.** I just laughed out loud.

# SEPTEMBER

## MONTH FORTY-SEVEN: Memories of Kure

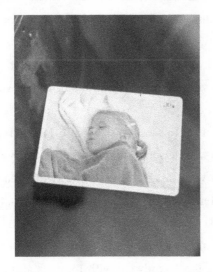

I was two, asleep on the sand near the Kure Beach Pier.

There are hundreds of photos from the past four decades in various stages of life. In looking through all of them, my favorite ones aren't of me, but of Parker or Hutch sleeping in the same way, on the same beach, near the same pier.

Every year this time rolls around; hurricane season. Every year there isn't a Hurricane Florence. She is a category 4 barreling north and east, and though she is getting weaker as I type this, she still has the potential to devastate that beach and pier and put the whole island underwater.

She could destroy everything . . .

But she can't take away the memories.

Tonight, those memories are flashing through my mind.

They begin with the small seaside cement-brick oceanfront cottage on Atlantic Avenue. My grandfather got it back in the '40s, as the beach town was starting to be established as a destination. It's right down from the Kure Beach Pier. The Grantham family has close to eighty years at this beach; no storm has ever made those cinder blocks move.

My dad taught me to coastal fish at Kure. I think I was five. That's when I used to wear a ribbon in my ponytail. Every year, my three brothers and I were dragged out of the twin beds in our house to walk to Easter morning sunrise service at 5:45 a.m. The greasy food place next to the pier has undergone lots of management changes, but long ago we'd watch Dad sit in a booth there and order a sausage toast sandwich with mustard and a side of grits. Southern to the core.

His ashes are in Kure's ocean.

So are my mom's.

They both have fish plaques you can buy as memorials that are embedded in the boardwalk. They're in different locations because they were divorced, but they both loved Kure, and it made sense to remember them on its beautiful shores.

An infamous Kure story goes that my youngest brother—who was still in diapers at the time—once ate a small cockroach as it crawled across his leg as he sat in our sandy shack. This is also the beach where all three of my brothers learned to surf. In high school, I'd do daily morning beach runs to train for field hockey, from the pier to the Atlantic Towers condo complex. It's the tallest structure permitted with beach zoning rules—thirteen stories high—and the trip is exactly three miles, round trip. Another brother had secret college parties in the cinder-block cottage, but he was also the one who, for Father's Day one year, surprise-installed a ceiling fan on the small screened-in porch. My grand-parents played Grantham Rummy on that porch for years. They had a running tally of victories. Nana Lolly was always beating Pop-Pop by about eighty games.

Wes and I got married there. Well, technically a few miles south at a gazebo in Fort Fisher, with the reception in Wrightsville, but we consider it an idyllic Kure Beach wedding week. We even had guests at the family cottage one evening for Eastern North Carolina barbeque.

Parker's first beach trip to Kure was when she was five weeks old. We waited until Hutch was a whopping four months. Kure is where Parker has become a mermaid and learned to boogie-board. It's where Hutch ate endless buckets of sand as a baby, and now jumps waves with fierce intensity.

They both did those things just last weekend. Just last Saturday and Sunday we were playing on Kure's coast.

My family has since sold our rusted cement-brick cottage, but I can still tell you every restaurant on the island, the best pizza, the one sushi place, where to get dive seafood and decent coffee. And Britts. Sweet, historic, glazed, melt-in-your-mouth Britts donuts. I dream of eating them while sitting in Charlotte on Sunday mornings.

Kure is my beach, and yours. It's ours. It's all of North Carolina's. Just like Wrightsville Beach and Carolina Beach and Oak Island, and every coastal town up to Corolla and Kitty Hawk, south through Hatteras and Morehead City and as far down as Sunset. If we cross the border, there's Myrtle and Surfside and Murrells Inlet, and always Charleston and its beautiful Isle of Palms. If Hurricane Florence doesn't directly hit one, it'll hit another. You don't want to feel relief in thinking the pattern shifts toward wiping out someone else. We're all impacted.

Last weekend, Florence was a category 2, aimed at "somewhere on the East Coast." By Monday morning, people were buying plywood and planning evacuations. She'd changed fast and had Wilmington in her sights.

All week, I've grappled with what people grapple with when they know there's nothing to really do, except hope.

So, here's to hope. Hoping for the best for everyone. For brick-lined downtown Wilmington first, and both Carolinas when Florence heads inland. It's not just about one beach, or one place, but I can't deny that just one is in my head. It feels good and right—it feels very real—to write the memories before Florence makes landfall hours from now, and then whatever happens, happens.

I feel Kure's grit. I feel her love. I can close my eyes and see every wooden plank of that pier I've walked probably 200,000 times.

She's a nasty storm, but stories in a soul can never be washed away.

*COMMENTS:*

**Donna V.** How beautiful. Made tears stream down my face.

**Lisa L.** Sunset Beach for us. Sold the house years ago to pay for two college educations. My husband is still there in an undisclosed dune; his wish. I'm guessing he's going to be relocated this weekend. I'm a little bummed but knew this day would come. We will have to do the plaque thing. Prayers for all in the path.

 **Molly.** Love "his wish."

**Donna B.** I love Kure Beach. My heart was heavy when I left our boarded-up house to wait on this ugly storm.

**Shelley Mc.** I'm right there with you. I went to UNC-Wilmington 22 years ago and have been going back as much as I can since. Something about that area stays in your soul.

**Drusilla N.** We were there Labor Day weekend. Hard to believe two weeks later it could be gone.

**Kim S.** I pray that our islands remain for more memories to be made.

**Susan H.** Love this. (From a resident of Wilmington who frequently visits Carolina Beach to actually get away.)

**Terry D.** My family all ended at Oak Island. My uncle and aunt built many cement block homes there. We are watching our security camera and not sure what to expect.

## Second Child Syndrome?

Guilt post. I forgot this little nugget has a birthday next week. The thought popped into my head twenty minutes ago while sitting at my desk reviewing newscasts. In a horrible but honest confession, I even found myself checking a calendar to make sure I knew what actual day he was born.

Once confirmed, I quickly emailed the mom of his little buddy with one hand, and called Chuck E. Cheese with the other. Problem solved. We'll have a small pizza lunch, big on excitement. He'll never know that I almost missed it completely.

Is this second child syndrome?

Even in this picture, the most recent one I could find on my phone, he's smiling sweetly, with no idea he's wearing a way-too-big jersey because why waste money on one that only fits now? He's wearing his sister's old soccer shorts because I have yet to buy him his own, and he's in shin guards and flip-flops because I forgot his real shoes.

Parker plans elaborate birthday events for herself, six months out. Then there's this kid.

I love you, Hutch-man. Please keep rolling with the flow.

---

*COMMENTS:*

**Della L.** You are so awesome for letting all the moms out here know we are human. And to make you laugh, my oldest son hit my daughter in the head with a frozen turkey while I was at work while they were growing up. Don't judge.

**Julie S.** What matters most is that you remembered and problem-solved. Timing not important.

**Penny C.** #1: You didn't forget! #2: It doesn't make any difference if it's planned 6 months out or day of. And #3: Don't get upset when he dresses like this as a teenager.

**Stacie S.** Molly, we are winning. Promise. He'll barely remember Chuck E. Cheese, but will remember feeling loved.

**Susan W. Y.** Blissfully unaware. Let him swipe a pass somewhere and he'll be fine.

**Ralph A.** I was the 4th child. Gets worse per kid. When I was yelled at, I was called every sibling name until mine.

## A Voice, a Bracelet, and the Weekend Ahead

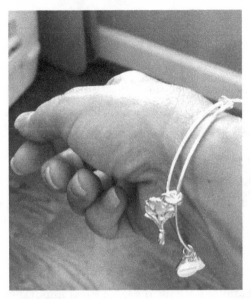

"I'm here to pick up my T-shirt."

From behind the table, her voice made me lift my head. Its sound hit inside my skull. I knew that voice. I knew it, but couldn't place it.

We caught eyes.

"Surprise, Molly."

*Oh my God. Oh my God!* "Melissa. What are you . . . wait?!? You signed up for our team?"

She kept smiling. "I wouldn't miss it."

I jumped—awkwardly leaped might be a better description—over the table and gave Melissa, my mom's hospice nurse, a huge hug.

Both of us had tears.

Melissa Pearson is one of a handful of hospice nurses who took care of my mom last May at the hospice house where Mom had her too-fast, unexpected stay. Those nurses were angels disguised as humans. Each one was exactly what you'd want for your final and worst moments of life. Each one—mostly women and one man—was sensitive, but strong. Straightforward but soft and full of patience and understanding.

Since then, I've run into a few of them out and about in life. They aren't just angels when walking hospice hallways; I think they're actually real everyday angels among us.

Take Melissa. Here she was standing in front of me at our Komen Charlotte Race for the Cure #TeamMolly T-shirt pick-up (I have a team every year to encourage people across the area to get involved in the fight against breast cancer), in the middle of the mall, an hour drive from her home.

"You didn't have to do this," I said. "You have a lot of patients. This is above and beyond."

"I'm doing this FOR all those patients," she said. "After your mom died you told me, 'We need to find a damn cure.' That's why I'm here. I want to help find it."

After Melissa got her shirt and left, I got to thinking.

I do often say "We need to find a damn cure," and believe—a way-down deep belief—that we will. Having hope in that belief is important.

But I'm not immune to how loss stings along the way.

I miss my mom. I miss my dad, who died of colon cancer back in 2006. Time has passed, yet I miss him every day. I miss my grandfather, who died of pancreatic cancer when I was in middle school. And none of my personal "missing" can possibly compare to the families who lose their kids to cancer. Every September, I write and share thirty stories of thirty amazing #MollysKids to help highlight Pediatric Cancer Awareness Month, and I think it's one of the most important things that can be done.

As I was there handing out T-shirts and thinking about finding a cure and the pain along the way . . . suddenly . . . Melissa was back.

"I went shopping," she said. "Just a little something."

In her outstretched palm was a square black box. She nodded, indicating I take it.

Inside was a beautiful silver Alex & Ani bangle, a bouquet of pink roses as its sole charm.

"Melissa . . . you didn't have to—"

She cut me off.

"It's not just for you," she said. "It's to remind you of all those you're fighting for."

If you look closely, you'll see Melissa's gift on my wrist while I'm on the news tonight. I've worn it every day since last weekend, and plan on wearing it Saturday morning as we kick off the start line, and at the Survivor Ceremony. Over 15,000 of us will be in Uptown Charlotte celebrating hundreds of current warriors who are winning their battles. I want the bracelet on my arm to represent them as much as it represents those who walk the route with us in spirit.

Melissa's gift is a shiny reminder of how real cancer is and why a cure is so desperately needed. She sees fragility every single day. And if she can keep hope, then we all can. I can and do.

I can't wait until we find that damn cure… until then, we'll keep rising, fighting and lifting up.

---

*COMMENTS:*

**Tess B.** In 2001, my mom was in a hospice facility. She was diagnosed with stage 4 ovarian cancer in December 1999. She had chemo and surgery but got to the point that there wasn't anything else they could do except manage her pain. The nurses in hospice were amazing. Thank you—I believe a breakthrough in any area will help all cancer research.

**Andrea R.** Reading your posts as I walk through my own cancer journey. I was recently diagnosed with Stage 3 colon cancer. At 37 years old. No history in my family and few symptoms. We must do our part to find a damn cure.

**Mike B.** Molly! You know how to make a man cry. Cancer is so evil, for both adults and children. Hope is still alive for a damn cure.

**Angela W.** My mother-in-law just passed yesterday after a 16-year battle with breast cancer in the hospice house. We were touched by several very special nurses . . . they are true angels. They treated her like their own family.

**Jeanie E.** I go tomorrow for my first mammogram since my breast cancer diagnosis. One year, I made it! I have seen and done things I never would have thought. Life is different now. I have learned to embrace a new normal.

**Carla F.** Nurses are special people . . . Hospice nurses are an exceptional breed.

**Tim Mc.** I will keep running every race, 5K, and fundraiser, until we find the damn cure.

**Jane S.** My husband and mother passed away at a hospice house. My husband, Randy, had colon cancer. In the time he was there he made lots of friends there especially with one Angel nurse Sally Rogers. They bonded as soon as we got there. Randy loved all the nurses there though, really, and so did I and still do. I still go back to visit them. They feel like family to me. They ARE Angels.

**Lydella P.** I'm on board with the tagline: #findadamncure

**Susan G. Komen Charlotte** Love this so much.

## The Real We Are

This picture was taken during my TEDx Talk last week. *(Internal monologue: Yes! I did a Tedx Talk! I got through it! And had fun!)* I wasn't going to mention it but changed my mind after thinking about it this weekend. I am proud of my message AND of the other speakers, and want to endorse the process.

All the other speakers I met through this journey—every single one of them—hit it out of the ballpark. Here's how it worked:

- Hundreds of Charlotteans applied to Tedx a year ago.
- About 140 were asked to audition.
- Seventeen were chosen as finalists.
- All finalists went through months of coaching, a grueling process. People were always on the verge of being cut.

- Tedx wanted to make sure that by the end, no one embarrassed themselves, or their brand.
- After a final audition, twelve went on stage last Friday.

My talk was called "The Real We Are." It had to do with the level of façade many of us put on in our professional lives and—for women especially—the armor we have to wear. How much of our lives can end up feeling like it's all just a role we play. But the real we are—the authenticity behind our masks—is what matters most.

Giving a Tedx Talk was a tough, fantastic experience. Each of us had an individual idea we wanted to share. One speaker focused on her famous father's Alzheimer's disease; one man talked about coming to grips with loving his little girl even after she grew up and told him she was a lesbian; another speaker talked about "The Insatiable Need to Try," while another focused on the power of music for women. I hung on her every word as she was talking through her own personal story, and how playing guitar saved her. She's now teaching her daughter that if she bands together with others girls, she'll find power in her own voice.

It's cool to hear different, well-mapped, passionate ideas. I was honored to be part of the lineup and hope, just maybe, the message of appreciating flaws, finding realness—practicing realness—and taking off the mask and costume a little more landed with some of you.

Watch my Tedx Talk at http://tinyurl.com/MollyTedxTalk.

## MONTH FORTY-EIGHT: Hallelujah, We've Hit Four

Whoever said "terrible twos" was WRONG. I recall having this fleeting thought with Parker years ago when she was three; nothing is fleeting about the thought with Hutch. It hits like a Mack truck a dozen times a day. I am over his love of the word no, and the dozens of militant unreasonable demands a three-year-old yells as daily conversation.

Not to say he's not funny. I mean, he's a funny kid. He knows it, we know it, and everyone who meets and hears him sees it in the work badges, routines, keys, cars, his obsession with his toy cash register and swiping pretend credit cards, taking imaginary lunch orders to play "Chick-fil-A," and how he watches cartoon episodes on repeat until he can quote every line.

Hutch's overall endearing quirkiness often leads people to say, "That kid is a good time."

BUT.

He YELLS. I preach "indoor voices," talk it through, ask him to "speak like a big boy." Nothing. No. It's all a scream. When he wakes up, when we do prayers at night, and you better believe when his sister gets something he doesn't (and unhelpfully rubs it in his face)—80 percent of what falls out of his mouth is at a high volume.

He's also adamant. Last week both he and Parker wanted to ride their scooters to the bus stop. No problem. Typical morning. Only while heading there that particular day, she fell hard and scraped up her hand and arm. As I was trying to mathematically figure the time it'd take to tend to her and whether I could still get her on the bus, Hutch slyly left us on the corner to go chase a little girl walking with her grandfather in the opposite direction.

He took advantage of my distraction. And knew it. Once I realized he was walking away, I ordered him back.

"HUTCH," I yelled, while kneeling on the ground with a slightly bloodied Parker. "GET BACK HERE."

But he didn't care. He heard me—he stopped and looked back at me and P. I knew by his body language he knew what he *should* do. But I also knew he wasn't going to do it. You can just sometimes tell with kids when they're going to take the other option. He smirked right at us, turned away, and sped off.

I became a madwoman. (I'm not proud, but whatever.) My tone was so impressively threatening, it made Parker stop crying, and she was the one with a legitimate reason to be upset. My voice hit Hutch's three-year-old ears a block away. He finally, slowly, returned to us, whining the whole time.

Good news: I didn't lose my mind. I just grabbed his wrist and locked him to my side.

Better news: This whole pantomime entertained Parker so much she forgot her pain. I was able to clean her up enough to push her on the bus, while whispering instructions to go straight to the school nurse for Band-Aids. Parenting at its finest.

Meantime, as I've struggled with how to handle three-year-old Hutch-isms, we've inched closer to his fourth birthday, and at the last minute, booked that small party at Chuck E. Cheese.

When we told him he'd have his own afternoon . . . to celebrate just him . . . his first party *ever*, despite the fact Parker has had one every year since birth . . . HE LIT UP. Every morning and night he'd shriek about the pizza and Chuck E. himself and gloat in Parker's face: "I get a pahhhhhrrrttttteeeeee. It's MY pahhhhhrrrttttteeee."

The morning of his party last weekend, I was outside on our front porch wrapped with a patchwork quilt and coffee. It was the first fall chill we've had, and I'd found twenty much-needed minutes of solitude.

As I sat gently rocking, it started to rain. A mist. The noise was soothing. For the first time in weeks, actual weeks, weight was slipping off my shoulders. The month of September had the #MollysKids campaign, starting school, Race for the Cure, two hurricanes, getting through a Tedx Talk . . . we were done. We'd done it all. These twenty minutes of peace were helping me feel the light at the end of the calendar-driven tunnel.

Then I heard him. Hutch. He was inside. Yelling (no surprise) for me. My heart sank. I gripped my coffee tighter as he toured the house, screaming my name, trying to find my hiding place so he could surely—I assumed with dread—bother and annoy me.

Finally, he saw my back through a window. Grunting with all his might, he opened the heavy front door and came outside dressed in nothing but a shirt, Batman underwear, and socks.

"MAMA!"

He pattered over. "Today is MY pahhhhhrrrrttttteeeee!"

"I know, Hutch," I said with zero excitement. "It is your day."

"MAMA, whatcha DOING?"

He was so *loud*. "Just sitting." He walked over and attempted to climb onto the porch swing. I begrudgingly lifted him while silently sighing. My quiet time was clearly done.

He scooted his feet under the blanket and lay back in my lap, still a perfect fit. His little body was warm, and his tangled translucent hair was right underneath my chin. He smelled good from his bath the night before.

"WHY are you outside, MAMA?"

"Because I wanted to be alone." No reason to lie.

"Why you wanna be alone, MAMA?"

"Because sometimes mommies need a break."

"WHY?"

"We just do, Hutch." He didn't say anything so I continued. "Sometimes you yelling and Parker fighting makes me want a break."

He wasn't listening and didn't acknowledge. Which was to be expected.

"Today is my paaahhhhhrrrrrtttttteeeee, MAMA."

I hugged him tighter. "I know it's your party, Hutch-Man. Are you going to get to see Chuck E. Cheese?"

"YES!"

"And do you get to play games?"

"YES!"

"Are you going to have pizza?"

"YES!"

"And what else?" I was trying to mindlessly carry the conversation, but my brain was fried.

"MAMA, I GET A PASS!"

Huh?

"MAMA . . . I GET A RED BIRTHDAY PAAAAAHHHHHHRRRRTTTTEEEEE PASS!"

My laugh erupted up out of my chest through both of us under that blanket.

"MAMA! I DO!" He thought my reaction was contradicting his statement. "I saw the pass ON TV!"

I'd seen the same Chuck E. Cheese commercial. That's what was so funny. The ad showed kids swiping plastic passes—no more tokens—to start games. No wonder he was so into this party.

It was then, as he was dreamily discussing his party pass, that I no longer wanted to be alone. I didn't want him to be older. I didn't want him to even be more soft-spoken or doting. I loved this little nugget, his messy hair, Batman Underoos, and the odd obsessions that fire cylinders in his mind.

"Oh, Hutch," I said. "I love you."

"I love you too, Mama," he said in a half-normal, nonyelling voice. "Today is my paaahhhhrrrttteeee. I'm now four. I'm a big boy."

We have a long way to go, but he's right. He really is getting to be one.

---

*COMMENTS:*

**Ellie G.** These moments are so perfect and precious. I can recall every single one with 1, 2, & 3. As badly as I wanted a break, I craved these one-on-ones with mine. The hectic everyday schedule, never ending whisper/yell, constant teasing, on-the-go dinner in the car, practice in 30 minutes, homework in the backseat, vocabulary words in the shower weeks, can never compare to a sweet little snuggle when you just need a break. I love reading how you do you. You are always so put together on TV. I love that you are just another mom like the rest of us.

**Kelly A.** I completely understand! My almost 4-year-old only has one volume (high) and one speed (fast). Everything she does is at top level. But she also loves bigger than any child. While it can be tiring to try and keep up; I wouldn't want her to be any different.

**Shannon H.** I felt like I was reading my own life with my 7-year-old son. But in the end, at the end of the day, it's worth it and I wouldn't trade it for the world.

**Denise C.** I'm a preschool teacher to older 3's . . . most just turned or are turning 4 and nope . . . inside voices are impossible.

**Angelita R** My life every day. Have a 6-and-3-year-old. The honesty is refreshing. I too, sometimes hide.

**Sherry S.** I love 4-year-olds!! I teach Kindergarten but 4 is my all-time favorite age. They are brutally honest. They are potty trained. They aren't tied to a school schedule yet. I love their curiosity, even though 12,345,678 questions a day will make you tired.

**Summer C.** I wish I had paid more attention and written down the small moments when they were little.

**Nicole R.** I am so glad to know that it isn't just my kids who can be heard 10 miles down the road every time they speak. This whole post spoke volumes (no pun intended) to me.

# NOVEMBER

## MONTH FORTY-NINE: Twitter Trolls

 4h
Replying to @MollyGrantham
Your rabid feminist, white female guilt is stunning. Always woven into every text. She'll never get one of us masculine men. Sad, sick.

43 views

♡2 ♺ ♡ ⬆

People are good. I say that often and believe it fully.

This weekend I found myself reacting to the other side of humanity.

I put a picture of Parker on Twitter—on Facebook as well—standing tall with a shirt that said *Girl Boss*. Her body language defined the message. I posted it as a mom who caught a glimpse of her daughter when her daughter didn't know she was looking. It was a seven-year-old with eyes locked ahead, shrugged-off jacket, posed atop a cement column, because if the column was there, clearly it was there to scale and own. From my critical eye as her mom, the bold lettering on the shirt was simply extra.

I posted the picture because, well, I can. It was Thanksgiving night. She's my daughter. I love her and was feeling grateful.

One fast reply came from a man with a made-up name and fake profile picture. He wrote: "Your rabid feminist, white female guilt is stunning. Always woven into every text. She'll never get one of us masculine men. Sad, sick."

He'd attached a photo of a bodybuilder kissing his muscles.

Out of habit, I hit Block. That's how many public people are trained to handle nastiness in social media; shake off your anger, don't reply, and keep going. So, I did. Took about ten minutes, but I moved on with the night.

But I woke up the next morning thinking about this particular troll. This one hit harder because he went after me AND my girl.

Everyone who lives and breathes journalism knows we're in a business where we better have thick skin. After two decades in this job, I've heard a lot of criticism and over-the-line comments. Because of that, I'm tough. I know how to handle hate.

But don't attack Parker.

Or Hutch, for that matter.

Especially with such unwarranted, unhinged language and some hypermasculine image.

So when I woke the next day, I thought. Hard. Through the whole first cup of coffee. Then I took a screen shot of what you see above and made it a diving board to jump into the following five tweets:

Why show you this? Because it's how some people think. Because this tweet is not rare. Because it's merely an example of venom I get sent directly . . . and it's by no means just me. Women everywhere get this stuff. We're told the messages are best to just ignore.

So 99% of the time, that's what we do. Ignore. Block and move on. But once in a while I think it's helpful to illuminate the insanity. Show the reality of some mindsets. Show the world what we take pains to NOT engage with.

Which is where I am this morning. Rather than just ignore the troll, I'm shining a flashlight on a deranged mindset so wrapped in fear and hatred, it'll pounce at any opportunity. Even an innocuous tweet about a 7-year-old.

That stuff is out there. Nasty messages trying to rattle don't need to actually hit, or ever hurt. Don't let them. But sometimes it's okay to call them out.

On that note, my next tweet is what really matters. Innocent goodness. I'm happily putting down my phone now. Going to focus on that the rest of the day.

My next tweet was this picture:

Then, with a clear mind, I put the phone down. I felt good.

∞

Twenty-four hours later I checked Twitter.

Many of you had responded.

Turns out this guy wasn't a new hater. Another reporter on Twitter (a male) tracked down his handle and said he'd been a troll to them before. I really appreciated that reporter's support. Other comments endorsed my decision to showcase his words and respond.

Let's be clear: we are living in a world where the majority of us put our lives out there. Now more than ever. You can choose to show whatever you want to show, but social media gives everyone a platform to endlessly show everything. Some like to keep it real; some like to Instagram-filter their lives away and create a fake sense of what is true. I am more in the first camp, choosing to show bits and pieces of my kids and write about the truth we're all living. To me, it seems silly to only show the TV-lit pretty images, being that 360 degrees of someone is what makes them full circle. But it's also one million percent fine if you choose to only show the good days or be completely private. That is an individual decision we can, and do, all make.

None of that is the disturbing issue.

The issue, I find, is the harsh judgment in response.

No matter what you choose to share or not share, or whether you choose to make it appear better and shinier than it may actually be, every stranger can have an opinion. On your kids. Your pets. Your family. Your words. Your look. Your opinions. Your beliefs. Your politics. The fact that people have opinions is nothing new, but now there are countless outlets that give strangers a place to throw their personal opinions about you—right toward your face.

I still think the best way to stop the nastiest of trolls is to block and ignore.

This weekend also taught me that addressing insanity can be rewarding.

That troll served the ball with no rules. He went after my daughter. I'd never in a million years consider volleying directly back to him and his low-class comment—I'd never give him that satisfaction—but I'd usually never retweet or share his comment either. It felt great this weekend to do so. I responded in a bigger-picture way, showcasing his cruel idiocy, with no direct communication to him at all.

I still think people are really good. We all see everyday examples. (#MollysKids alone is constant proof. The big hearts of those of you who look for those stories, and network together to help lift up kids in our community, is overwhelming. I see and absorb your words, comments, gestures, actions, and kindness almost weekly.) But when the other side appears, like this weekend, maybe a protective Mama Bear shouldn't always stay seated.

You have no idea how much I appreciate the grace you guys give here to let life be lived through words. Thank you. I don't always know the turns months will take, but I know I can write about them and learn something along the way.

---

*COMMENTS:*

**Gale C.** I loved that original picture of Parker. I'm reposting it here to remind us all of innocence, beauty and strength all rolled into one.

**Neal C.** Unfortunately Molly, there is a tremendous amount of hatred in this world. As a parent of two special needs boys, I see it more than I care to. It's not easy to turn the other cheek when insults are hurled at our precious children.

**Elizabeth E.** What matters? Parker & Hutch. They matter. This d-bag has no sense of boundaries. He clearly stepped over with the intention of attacking you being a mom. Your instincts to fire back are 100% justified. I'm glad you addressed it.

Your posts of the kids are simplicity in a chaotic world. They show you are a mom and proud of your children. You share your kids with all of us, and we (I know I do for sure) love you and those littles. Watching them grow up over the past 5+ years is awesome.

**Kim O.** First, feminist is NOT a dirty word. I should know. I am one and a I'm also a real life boss. Parker is lucky to have a bad a$$ mama to emulate. Move on troll.

**Connie S.** I hope you can read my daughter's shirt. If not, it reads, BELIEVE WOMEN. I hope I have taught her how to be independent and strong. Be proud of your daughter. It's hard for me to ignore trolls, but I'm learning to do better by not engaging in any debate.

**Richard P.** A sign at my office says, "Can't fix stupid." Keep on keeping it real.

**Mark J.** Ignorance and just plain old meanness seems to run rampant. I think the ability to remain anonymous feeds the actions.

## Xmas List

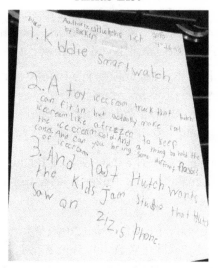

Received a Santa list on dinner break. Hutch let his older sister "authorize" (where does he get these words?) as he dictated. He's not getting #1 and I have no idea what #3 is. Shame he's not specific on #2.

Maybe I can use the magical North Pole pass from last year to swipe myself into the workshop and ask all those elves how to pull this one off?

---

*COMMENTS:*

**LaLa D.** Hutch definitely needs his own ice cream truck.

**Karyn C.** Awww, come on. That would be awesome. With a key card to start it!

**Victoria H.** Girl, you are in for a long next 15 years.

## A Shepherd

First preschool play. I'm melted.

---

*COMMENTS:*

**Heather M.** Did he have a card to swipe to enter the manger?

 **Molly.** Oh. He was required to take the badge he wore to preschool today off for the play.

**Elliot F.** Give him a lightsaber and he'd look like a Jedi.

## Push-Ups, Panthers, and an Ice-Cream Truck Tour

Santa delivered. As best he could. Hutch squealed with delight yesterday morning upon seeing the motorized ice-cream truck beneath the tree. Opened the plastic door, sat down, and pounded the mini steering wheel with gleeful noises, eyes scrunched together with laughter.

Twenty-four hours later, it was a beautiful day-after-Christmas afternoon. The kind of Carolina day where you don't need jackets. Instead of riding his sister's scooter or begging us to take him on a bike, he used all his might to heave the ice-cream truck out onto the side porch stoop, determined to head out to find customers.

Off we went. Parker, Hutch, Fisher, Wes, and myself. On a "walk" to sell pretend ice cream.

Never could Santa's dedicated workshop leaders have predicted

the intensity of Hutch's sense of responsibility
for his vehicle. He owned this thing. None
of us could get near him, not even Fisher
the dog, who is often the universally favorite
family member.

It took Hutch a couple of blocks to figure
out how to keep the steering wheel straight to avoid going in circles
or weaving off the sidewalk. But by the time we got on the back
road through a park toward Uptown, this little nugget vendor was
untouchable. Cruised right by Bank of America Stadium with such

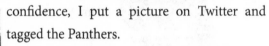

confidence, I put a picture on Twitter and
tagged the Panthers.

We went through a parking lot. Down busy
Mint Street. Up past Romare Bearden Park and
past the Charlotte Knights stadium. Right into
the heart of the city.

Hutch waited at red lights before crossing—
driving—in the pedestrian walk. Anyone he passed laughed and
hit the person they were with to assure they, too, had witnessed

a child driving a plastic ice-cream truck
through busy downtown streets. He nodded
at a few people, but for the most part was
looking ahead at whatever was next. His
hands were at ten and two, like a legit driver,
with a four-year's-old expression showing a
mixture of joy and confidence.

Meantime, Wes and I hung behind, watching, internally dying. Only Hutch.

Finally, he said he was hungry. We directed him toward a brunch spot. He pulled right up and parked that truck diagonally, blocking the cement steps that led to the front door, and headed inside the restaurant. Apparently, you get VIP parking if your car is three feet long.

While eating I checked my phone. The Panthers had seen my tweet and responded.

"We'd like to purchase some. Does he have any Push-Ups left?"

Hutch, thrilled at the prospect of a customer and more determined than ever, quickly wrapped up brunch for us to return the way we came. Parker was also excited, and Wes and I were simply praying that the ice-cream truck battery lasted. Off we went, back into the heart of the city, past Knights' stadium, Romare Bearden Park, up busy Mint Street, through a parking lot.

Approaching the Carolina Panthers practice field, Hutch drove right by three dozen NFL fans waiting outside the metal barriers with footballs and pens and scraps of paper, hoping to get just one player to come by. Drove right by. As if he owned this compound. He cruised up the sidewalk to the practice gate, about to open any minute and release over seventy massive men.

He parked beside that front entrance and sat down on the truck's little chair. Suddenly, the gate widened. He sat up straighter, sensing an influx of ice-cream questions.

Netting that blocks your vision into the practice field was removed, and players in sweaty jerseys, holding helmets and equipment, filed out. Practice was over.

Every one of those athletes and staff members walked right by Hutch and his little truck. He remained silent. I think his four-year-old self was hoping that if words were in his head, people could hear them. Thinking, praying, mentally begging, for someone to stop to "buy" pretend ice-cream.

But of course, no one stopped.

"Hutch, say something," I finally pushed. "Ask them if they want any ice cream."

"NOOOOOO." He sounded scared, and still sitting in his truck, turned to me looking nervous as could be.

And then . . .

. . . #58 Thomas Davis, former Walter Peyton Man of the Year, family man and team captain, looked in the direction of that low wail. He put two and two together in a flat second, broke from the pack, and walked toward Hutch.

"I'll take a . . ."

Surprising all of us, Hutch hopped up from his truck to run back toward me. Rather than leave, Thomas—who knew kids and shyness—cracked a joke. "Oh, well then," he said as he reached down to grab Hutch's vehicle. "I'll just take the whole truck then."

Hutch ran back to his prized Santa gift protectively.

"It's mine," he said to the defensive linebacker.

"Does it play music?" Thomas asked.

Hutch hit the bell jingle.

That's all it took. Just like that, they were friends. I have video of the whole interaction, but not one photo. This is a screengrab from the video clip. Thomas gave Hutch a high five; Hutch seemed to feel as big as the many men he'd watched just pass him by.

On the way home, Hutch stopped for a bathroom break.

When he got back into the truck, the battery was dead. Wes carried that truck on his head the rest of the walk home, as Hutch skipped ahead, bragging to his sister about his new buddy who wears the numbers 5 and 8.

3.4 miles.

2.5 hours.

Zero cones sold.

Overall, a stupendous tour.

## MONTH FIFTY: The Lesson of Legos

They are under my feet every second, should be a part of torture chambers, and have no good way to truly be stored.

But what a brilliant toy. Or brilliant projects. Or brilliant over-priced obsessions. However they're classified, someone is doing something right in how they design, market, and sell these plastic pieces. They're stupendous time-suckers, can act as a babysitter, and are a constant teacher. Dozens of Lego contraptions have given Parker mental engineering workouts better than any parent or class ever could.

Notice I said Parker. They haven't helped Hutch.

That's where I am this morning.

How can Lego sets be naturally easy for certain kids . . . and quantam physics for others?

Parker started with big Lego Duplo blocks for chubby toddler hands at the age of two. She had a "girl" set, pastel in color. (SIDEBAR: Why do toy manufacturers make all girl things pink and all boy things not-pink, as if we're determining girls can't like science or engineering, and boys shouldn't play with dolls?) She'd build tall towers, then knock them over. By age three, she was stacking horizontal floors to create depth, and by age 4, was pouring over the Lego catalog that miraculously showed up at our house. (SIDEBAR 2: Big Brother companies always seem to be watching to know what you'll buy.)

For Christmas when she was five, Parker wanted the Disney Magic Kingdom castle for age 16+ with over 4,000 pieces and 360 pages of instructions. Santa brought it. I mentioned the castle when we went to Disney—how in awe she was to see it towering in front of her. That's because she'd only seen it in Lego form. Santa thought it'd be good to test this precocious five-year-old. Show her how there are always bigger mountains, and a challenge is good.

Silly Santa. He should've known better. Parker opened that Lego box Christmas morning and started immediately. Right there on the big table in the living room. Every morning she'd work with her head down and eyes alert. When kindergarten started again, she'd work in the afternoons. Occasionally she would ask us—Mom or Dad—for help in finding a particular piece, but for the most part, she was determined to do that darn thing herself.

She finished Valentine's Day, not two months later. It was a testament of what devotion can accomplish. It remains on display in our living room as a proud reminder to her—and a daily slap in the face to Santa—to never doubt dedication.

All of this is a long example to say that Parker's mind can solve a Lego.

By contrast, this picture shows Hutch's interest: trying, sort of, to fit together big starter-set Duplo blocks and wholly stumped by the directions. He's two years past the age when Parker could do these with her eyes closed.

Recently watching him casually care about a baby Lego set was an eye-opening moment for me. The only path I had in my head was of a child who connected them easily. And here he was . . . struggling . . . and only half-caring. Yet, Hutch is smart. He's wicked smart. His mind stumps us in its laser focus of things, its ability to remember one-liners from movies and songs, his long-term retention of phone passwords or the way he'll recall directions from the back seat to a place he's been once.

As I sat here quietly watching him, I realized a simple statement, but one easily forgotten:

Different children learn in different ways.

As he stared at that directions page, I stared at him. The Lego book had him perplexed; his confusion showed that learning abilities might shift as you age, but apparently by age two some children can follow linear directions, and some, like Hutch, have more creative, non-traditional, quirky interests (say, badges that beep and give access).

The way you think must be set very early on. To me, not a

scientist, seeing two kids with the same DNA play with the same toy in polar opposite ways with distinctly separate learning curves is a true anecdotal *aha*.

And, teachers. As if we needed to respect you anymore. You have a classroom full of minds, learning different ways, and you have to get them on the same page.

As I write this—I'm not kidding—Parker has woken up and sat beside me at that big living room table. It was the workshop for the Disney castle two years ago and ever since has become a Lego city of sorts. As I've been typing, she has been working on making what the box calls "Heartlake Hospital." It only has 871 pieces, so my guess is it'll be done by lunch. She wants to finish that one, she said, before starting on the 2,464-piece Ferris wheel "expert" level that Santa brought her this year as her big gift.

In the meantime, Hutch is sprawled on the couch, blaring a cartoon, with his hands in the cereal box, a police pass around his neck and a full Pull-Up still on. He couldn't be happier.

Both are living their best lives. Just very different ones.

*COMMENTS:*

**Nell W.** I love that you recognized the challenge teachers face every single day. Children learn in different ways and at different ages, in varying amounts of time . . . However, our testing methods expect them to reach goals at the same time. It just doesn't make sense. As a retired school principal, I could stay on this subject forever. Children need to be able to learn when they are developmentally ready to learn.

**Malinda C.** I wish I could like this a million times! It is so true. Amazing that siblings can have the same DNA and be so different.

**Helms L.** How boring life would be if we were all the same.

**Terry J.** This difference was apparent to me after years of home-schooling. They all learn differently and at different paces, but all 6 of my kids are successful adults in their own ways.

**Julie C.** I have said for years that Lego marketing strategy was the most genius ever. When we were young, they were simply squares & rectangles. It worked for our time. Now we parents spend $149 for ONE kit to build ONE thing, and in most families, they end up in jumbled piles after the initial build . . .yet we go buy another kit with the latest must-have theme. Brilliant.

### Parker Pal Note

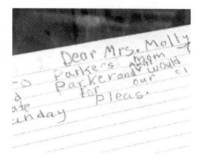

Excuse me as I choke on laughter over the note for "Mrs. Molly" sent home with Parker from a friend. They'd "like a play date on Sunday, Pleas." Bold, polite, resourceful: here's to finding creative paths to getting done what we want to accomplish.

### Easy-Bake Oven

Four braids. Two princesses. One Easy-Bake Oven.

# JANUARY

## MONTH FIFTY-ONE: Win vs. Fail

WIN: Giving yourself twenty extra minutes to sleep.

FAIL: When your boy takes your naptime as a chance to find scissors and give himself a haircut.

---

*COMMENTS:*

**Summer C.** My daughter did that. Cut the entire side of her hair all the way around to bang level. This is a pic of her bowl cut that resulted . . . her hair was shoulder-length before.

**Tiffany S-H.** My daughter decided the day before school picture day to give herself a new do. I made her go that way because I had no money for haircut. She had cut it off above the ear on one side, the other was very long. She never did it again and I have a permanent picture to remind us both of that day . . . I think all kids go through this stage.

**Charles T.** When I was in first grade I saw Edward Scissorhands. There was a scene where Mr. Depp is styling hair. Sometime after that, I gave myself a haircut in the middle of class. My teacher and my mom were not thrilled.

**Kelly R.** Molly, you cannot leave us hanging. Picture of his artistry please!

# FEBRUARY

## MONTH FIFTY-TWO:
### Look Familiar? Round Two.

It's not the dress that I notice. Not the sneakers or random leggings or the scab on her chin from when she fell off her hoverboard and hopped back on, still bleeding.

It's the eyes.

It's the look.

The sassy half smirk of a smile that silently screams: "Are you with me or not?"

ᎧᎸᎤ

For those who remember the black dress escapade from two Christmases ago (she's wearing the dress on the cover of *Small Victories*), this is what you could call Round Two: Valentine's Day. Only this episode has a much different ending.

We were in the same consignment boutique. She and her brother were hanging with me in the dressing area as I sped through outfits at Mach 10. A trip where you are simply and quickly trying on what you need—not any actual shopping enjoyment. After last year's Mother's Day debacle, I don't go in anywhere with them unless the place is virtually empty, so this was a breeze. Parker said she wanted to go look at what was in the store. It's a contained, lovely shop. I knew she'd be safe. I said fine.

She soon returned to the dressing room area, and through the curtain, said she was getting in another booth to try something on.

I had a flash. A transport back in time to when she had a complete meltdown in this very same store over a black dress that was nineteen sizes too big for her, and I died ten thousand deaths of embarrassment.

*But it was fine*, I told myself. *No need to panic over a meltdown that hasn't happened in this current moment. You're fine.*

So, as my fiery mind calmed itself down despite the memories keeping it pulsed, I told her okay.

"Sure, P. Just be careful not to mess anything up."

Two minutes later she said she was dressed. Asked me to pull back her curtain and look in her room.

This.

She said nothing. I said nothing. She looked at me. Didn't flinch, didn't utter a word, didn't uncross her arms.

In no way was I getting her a dress that wasn't her size and too expensive—again—and let it hang in her closet. Instead, I took a picture. Gave me time to think about how to proceed.

"Can I get it?"

"No."

"Why not?"

I stared back. Played her game.

Didn't blink, didn't talk, didn't act like I cared.

"Okay," she said suddenly with a shrug in her voice. "I knew you'd say no. I just wanted to show you. Aren't the sparkles pretty?"

Humor laced her tone. Without actually saying it, she was making sure I knew the joke was on me. Our dressing room disaster from over two years ago was obviously in her sharp little mind as well . . . only this time, she didn't think the fight was worth it.

Her understanding of the moment and maturity in the discussion almost made me want to say, *Okay sure! Let's get it!* (Isn't it funny how if your kids don't whine, it makes you want to go back on convictions and give them everything?)

Instead, I chose a smarter response. "The sparkles are beautiful, P. I love your sense of style in picking these things out."

"I just wanted to show you, Mommy. I'll take it off now."

*What alien took my girl?*

CℨℬↃ

I remain constantly perplexed and stunned and thrilled and over-whelmed with awe and pride for this seven-going-on-eighteen-year-old.

As a tip for your future, P, keep that look on your face. Confidence is stunning, no matter what it's dressed in.

---

*COMMENTS:*

**Debbie B.** I hope you are still writing updates when she is 13-14.

**Stacey C.** Love that last line . . . that's a game changer!

**Elizabeth N.** Courage . . . that's what I'm reading woven through your words. She "knew" what the outcome would be, yet she showed much courage by facing you head on and not worrying about what your reaction would be.

## Window Surprise

1) Thank you for a child who writes surprise messages I see when the blinds are raised after she's at school.
2) Thank you for a child who also understands I'll wonder what pen/Sharpie/crayon was used and instead of making me ask later, leaves soapy cleaner in the sink.

Happy Valentine's Day.

# MARCH

## Mood

The face of someone desperately trying to not celebrate Sunday Funday.

---

*COMMENTS:*

**Darren R.** We all have our days where we are just not feeling it.

**Steve M.** You say that's Hutch but how do we know that's really Hutch?

**Angel W.** Future investigative reporter.

## MONTH FIFTY-THREE: Daylight Saving Time

They think losing an hour on the clock means waking up earlier to gain an hour of playtime.

Also, I'm tired. Too much this month. That's all I have. As honest as it gets. Sorry. Kids are exhausting.

---

*COMMENTS:*

**Rogers W.** Not unanimous smiles.

**Susyn W.** His bangs are growing back!

**Chris L.** That kid is a good time even when he loses an hour.

**Miller W.** Oh yeah, they are ready to rock n roll.

**Britton M.** Don't worry. We parents get it.

## Checklist

Everything. Must. Be. Just. Right. Or. Else.

NOTE: Happened to be Wear Green Day. Of which—no surprise—I had no idea. But walked in, looked around and—Bam! His electric lime green shoes counted. Sometimes it's better to be lucky than good.

*COMMENTS:*

**John A.** Wait just a minute here. Spiderman? Avengers lunchbox? You're getting ready to have the best time of your life. Ages 7-12 is the best. I went to eat lunches with mine at school. School dances and fall festivals . . . try to go to all of them. I coached baseball for 10 years. My bosses would say, "You're missing so much overtime." Money won't buy memories. I had me some fun. I was 30 before I started a family. Just keep 'em in whatever and every after-school activity as you can find.

**Dee L.** When my son-in-law was in elementary school his Mom totally missed the costume date. She dressed him in a beagle costume, only to find out while standing at the bus stop with the kids pointing and laughing, it was the wrong day. Poor thing.

**Abby C.** God, I love how you let both of those kids just be their own style.

# APRIL

## MONTH FIFTY-FOUR: Personalities in a Photo

Been a while. At least it feels that way to me. A while since I've really stopped to look at my kids. We talk every day. We argue and compliment and hug and love. But I haven't stopped to study them recently. Haven't documented much (or so it feels) more than a few quick one-liners.

I'm sorry. Not really to you guys reading . . . I'm apologizing to Parker and Hutch for later in life. The absolute beauty of writing now is that they'll know details of their childhood and—this is important—so *I* don't forget the memories.

But as any writer knows, the truth of the matter is you have to be inspired. Last weekend we went to a zoo in Carolina Beach, on a not-so-warm spring break day, and I turned and saw them playing on this statue.

If that's not her.

If that's not him.

The image washed over and makes me want to remember this slice of who they currently are in life.

P first.

At just-turned-eight, she's still young, but older than I sometimes assume. She sees and understands things on her own. Her stories about social situations at recess and what she finds funny from inside her classroom provide insight into a girl who's not a child but far from a teenager. She's a rule follower. A child learning to mature through meltdowns faster than before, one who naturally uses manners during meals or when asking for something, and like many girls, goes up and down on wanting to tell me things.

For instance, the answer to "How was your day?" can range from one curt word to a twenty-minute diatribe on what so-and-so said, which math problems in class were easy, how she wishes she had more bathroom breaks, the reason a current dance move is hard to learn, and, in order, the names of the people who placed first through eighth in relay races organized on the playground. She says she beats the boys, an oddly rewarding, pride-bursting feeling inside me.

She's an extroverted homebody who knows what direction she'll take no matter who follows behind.

Normally, the follower is Hutch.

Enter this picture.

Hutch follows, but as I've said before and hopefully have chances to say again, he has distinct traits and is his own person. He is hands-down the happiest child you've ever met. He hums when he walks. Or bounces. Or skips. Sometimes, a combination of all three. We call him "Happy-Happy-Hutch" or "Too Much Hutch," because he's always extra. His unique addictions with things no longer surprise anyone—passes and keys and his ice-cream truck. Lately, he loves bath bombs. (The Easter Bunny today brought him a big jar of small blue square fizzy ones.) I mean, *bath bombs*?? But that's the beauty of Hutch. He is wholly unpredictable.

Not only can you never guess what he'll attach himself to, you also can't predict what hysterical words will drop from his four-year-old mouth. Things like how he responds to every statement we say with the question, "Are you serious?" or "Wait . . . WHAT???" And then there's his talent of describing entire plots, characters, and costumes for intricate Disney musicals. He still is using a high-pitched shriek with his tiny teeth showing to talk through conversations, and he often yells things only to end the discussion by running from the room to leave you laughing over his clever childish humor.

His memory is intense. Even more than Parker's, who doesn't forget a thing.

He is loving, entertained at all times, and happy to be in her world.

Together, they're logic meets magic.

And I feel tons better writing it down for the ages.

---

COMMENTS:

**Julie G.** I believe your posts help some of us to remember to pause and appreciate the moments with our families despite our schedules.

**Cyndi K.** I wish I had done what you have done with your digital journal for my two girls. Now I believe I will do it for my grandchildren.

**Gloria L.** As I watch my grandkids, as they grow up too fast, sometimes it's just the little things that catch you and you just want to keep them little longer.

**Susan W.** Love reading about the meltdowns as well as the good times.

## Fort Fisher Hermit

Time for a story. Little out of nowhere, but it just randomly crossed my desk and I'm sharing it to cross yours.

Maybe you've heard of the Fort Fisher Hermit? With my long love of Kure Beach, I recall him referenced in a vague way, but never knew much more than he was an old guy who lived in Fort Fisher long ago. I wasn't even sure if he was real or a passed-down fable.

Then I got these photos in the mail at the station yesterday.

Charles McCall, from Stanfield in Stanly County, sent four black-and-whites in an envelope. No letter. No explanation. Just old photos sent to me at WBTV News on the envelope. One photograph had writing on the back indicating that Charles was an eight-year-old boy in one of the pictures.

I was thoroughly confused, until moments ago.

While at my work desk cleaning out emails, I saw one I thought I'd deleted from this week. The only thing the person wrote was, "I thought you might like reading this link about the beach you love." I never clicked the link in the email—we're warned from clicking links because people sometimes intentionally send computer viruses to journalists—but I now saw the person who sent the email was named "Charles."

It seemed too coincidental. Two Charleses trying hard to reach out. I took a risk and clicked the link.

The link was an article about the man in the pictures sent in the actual mail: the Fort Fisher Hermit. Turns out his real name was Robert E. Harrill. The article quoted information presented at a Kure Beach town meeting back in 1995. According to the article, Robert's life was a true tale.

He was born in Shelby on February 2, 1893. His mother and two brothers died in the early 1900s from typhoid fever. His father remarried, and his stepmother was very dominating and strict. All of this about a real man I'd always thought was legend. The article said:

> His childhood was cut short and he grew up in an atmosphere of family violence. He often sought solitude into the woods or into nearby streams, rivers and lakes . . . He attended Boiling Springs High School and later returned to the school when it became Gardner-Webb University (when it was Gardner-Webb Junior College) to study ministry. In 1913, he married a girl

*named Katie. They had five children. Four sons and one daughter, who died shortly after birth.*

I'm summarizing here, but it seems Robert's family thought he was disturbed. They felt his problems were caused by the abuse he suffered as a child, and those problems caused the family to break up in the 1930s. Katie took her children to Pennsylvania. Robert made a living peddling trinkets and making jewelry, such as ID bracelets.

Eventually, at the age of sixty-two, Robert moved into a World War II bunker near Fort Fisher. He lived there for seventeen years. Ultimately, his fame grew—I mean, how many beaches have a real-life bearded hermit who lives in a bunker?—and he became one of the biggest tourist attractions on the Carolina/Kure/Fort Fisher island.

The article explained it this way:

> *He made like he didn't like the popularity when all these people kept coming to see him. However, HE painted 'The Fort Fisher Hermit' on a pillar to the entrance of the road to the bunker.*

Robert died in June of 1972. Some say of natural causes, but the article said others suspected foul play. He was buried in a cemetery in Shelby, but later was moved to the Federal Point Cemetery on Dow Road in Carolina Beach.

Charles, I'm not sure why you sent me all this, but thank you. My next mission is to see if the bunker is still there. I'd like to go see it, just out of piqued curiosity.

*COMMENTS:*

 **Molly.** I made a short link to the article Charles sent that has the historical facts about the Hermit, in case you're interested in reading more: https://tinyurl.com/FtFisher-Hermit. There's also an hour-long documentary at https://www.youtube.com/watch?v=qyJaF1EBTlU.

**Terry S.** I think I still have the book [on him]. My uncle used to visit him. Sad ending.

**Sharon H.** WOW. I have never heard of this before but enjoyed reading it.

**Larry B.** I remember him as a kid, our family always stayed in Kure Beach and had to take a trip down to Fort Fisher to see him. Those photos bring back memories of the good ole days.

**Lisa C-L.** Robert Harrill has always been part of my family history. He was my grandmother's, Lela Harrill Davis's, uncle. I was just sharing his story with a coworker at The Shelby Star on Thursday and told him I should send it to you! Was astounded to wake up and see your story today. The bunker is still very much there. My mom and daughter just visited several years ago. There has also been a book written on him, a TV documentary, and The Fort Fisher Hermit Society was founded in 1993 partially by one of his sons, my cousin, Edward Harrill and his wife Vergie. If you go to their website, you can view the documentary. Thank you for bringing his story back to light. As folks age and pass away, stories like his and little pieces of our history tend to fade, too.

## Girls' Night

Saturday, sushi, and teaching her to play the greatest game ever.

---

*COMMENTS:*

**Steven J.** Makes me wish my kiddos were young again.

**Donnell K.** Monopoly. Will challenge you (and her?) anytime.

**Nathan H.** My favorite game also!

# MAY

## Cast Dinner

The juggle is real. That's not a typo. I don't mean *struggle*. It's a juggle. Period.

There is no way to accurately describe the balls a parent keeps up in the air when they have a career and raise kids. Many of you understand. It's a constant rotation of trying to catch one ball, quickly deal with whatever that ball is, then tossing it back up so you have a hand free to catch whatever ball is next heading down. Some days you drop a few. That's okay. You learn to accept. You have to, because the reality is you *can't* do it all. You can try, but you'll never be able to hold all the balls at once. So, you learn. You adjust. You switch back and forth. You realize one day might be 95 percent filled with juggling balls that deal with family and life, and only 5 percent job . . . and the next day filled 90 percent with balls about your work, and only 10 percent with the rest of life. So, you pick one ball in given moments, and the next day or week another one gets your attention.

Some balls—especially if you work an odd shift like 2 p.m. to midnight—you leave on the ground permanently. Like, for me, the ball labeled "parent-involvement-in-after-school activities."

Through all this, you keep going. Keep juggling and catching and tossing back up to focus on the next thing coming. You do this because that is the only way to keep the entire act in motion.

Every once in a while, you get caught up in a moment and feel compelled to sign up and add in a new, temporary, ball. I did that tonight. Parker's drama club needed a dinnertime taco bar for seventy-five kids. It was the same exact time as my dinner break from work. And baby, that was all me. I signed up last week excitedly. I was going to do a mom activity! I then called in the order, planned the pick-up down to a five-minute window, anchored a few shows, rushed to the restaurant, packed up my car with pounds of black beans and hot queso in chafing dishes, and arrived at the school. TV makeup and all. I think I scared half the kids.

Little background: the K–fifth graders I fed tonight are putting on *The Lion King* this weekend. Parker auditioned back in the fall and landed the part of Young Nala. There's a large cast, and the rehearsals were way more involved than you might assume for an elementary-school performance. A local production company partners with her school and comes in for eight months, practicing the blocking, dancing, singing, and acting with the kids.

Anyway, the next three nights of final rehearsals are starting off on the right foot: the director wanted her seventy-five student thespians to have full stomachs.

In my eagerness to be the parent in charge of the taco bar, I never thought how I'd be scooping out beans onto paper plates as the news spun on, smack in the middle of my work day. So there I was, asking elementary school kids if they wanted "pinto or black?" while A) counting every long second they took to decide, and B) simultaneously wondering when the calls I'd made to the police department about three dangerous armed robberies would be returned. We were hoping to get surveillance video to show at 11 p.m., and ask officers if the robberies were connected. I'd mapped them, and they were within two miles and three hours of each other. It seemed a natural question despite no officer being willing—at least so far—to address the answer.

Even if they called back now, I couldn't pick up. That's what I kept thinking. I had queso on my forearms, bits of rice stuck to my cheeks, and both hands were in plastic gloves slopping out food on paper plates.

Fast forward an hour, and I'm washing black bean sauce out of my fingernails while reviewing news scripts. I'm still waiting for call backs from the police—I should text them, too, I think—and, feel successful while mentally jumbled. The juggling balls are still in rotation.

See you guys in ninety minutes on the news. If you see pico on my dress, give me a pass.

---

*COMMENTS:*

**Richard V.** "The juggle is real." Think you just wrote the title to your next book. Market that and put it on t-shirts. My wife and all of her friends would understand and wear proudly.

**Brittany W.** The best little brother ever? Did he get a key to get inside the school doors? LOL.

 **Molly.** He didn't understand why he couldn't serve ice cream out of his truck.

## Instagram Reminders

"See your post from two years ago."
Phew. Miss you, Mom. Here's to hand-holding and love.

---

*COMMENTS:*

**Helen H.** You will discover a part of your Mom lives on in you.

**Michelle R.** I miss my mom too. My second Mother's Day without her.

**Brad B.** Picture of love. No words needed.

## Proud and Exhausted

In the past twenty-four hours, she was Young Nala, nailed two two-hour dance recitals, and received a surprise Rising Star award while on stage from her dance studio. She showed up at tonight's drama club production clutching a stuffed animal of the lioness she portrayed while still wearing the dance company tank top. It has been an insane day. This is the perfect picture. I love how she loves it all.

PS: Today was my birthday. No one remembered, least of all me. Somewhere along the way, your days turn into theirs.

## New Pass

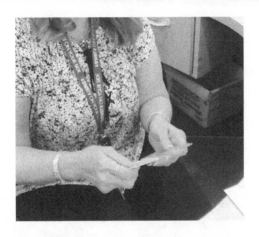

Kathy works at our station's front desk. She is making me a new pass—once again—because Hutch took my actual security-approved work badge, then lost it. Or hid it. Or something. Which means today, for the umpteenth time, I walked into Kathy's lobby, looked at her with no words, and she started clearing out my old security listed in the system and started making me a card for new access. She didn't question; I didn't have to ask. This is the dance Kathy and I have played for going on two years.

For everyone who said, "He'll grow out of it"—I'm still waiting.

---

*COMMENTS:*

**Wendi K.** I think we all have that person we play some "dance" with at one time. Believe it or not you are someone's dance partner too. Most of your dance partners are probably 3-4 ft tall.

**Suzi H.** Bless Hutch.

## Not Worth the Argument

They picked their own outfits today. This is what he wore to school.
#TooMuchHutch

---

*COMMENTS:*

**Wendilynn S.** Goofy faces and nonsense. Beautiful.

**Richard J.** Embrace uniqueness and individuality.

**Catherine A.** Must be Super Girl to lift up Spiderman!

## Newsroom at Night

Nothing to see here. Nothing at all. Please don't mind Hutch falling asleep in a fort in the newsroom. Reporter Amanda Foster doesn't seem to mind. She's able to focus on her own work with no concern that a four-year-old is sleeping on the floor.

Thank you to my always awesome team of coworkers for rolling with the punches when dinnertime childcare gets crisscrossed and my kids come to work for an hour. Tonight Hutch got sleepy, and Parker fell in love with intern Maya. All in a day's (evening's?) work.

*COMMENTS:*

**Katie H.** You are so lucky you get to bring your kiddos to work. I have to call out, unfortunately, when we have childcare conflicts.

**Garrett G.** Sleep is important . . . life events around you not so much. And Parker is in training for your job Molly, beware.

**Wanda R.** Hutch adapts to anything. Another Small Victory for sure.

**Roman C.** I used to take mine when I had to work on Saturday and took a sleeping bag and toys. Great memories.

**Preston A.** It's great your coworkers are clearly also friends and adjust to the zig and zag for family.

## Land of the Free

Memorial Day. Spacious skies and open space. Thank you.

# JUNE

## MONTH FIFTY-FIVE: True Love, Forever

Thank God we're in June. May needs to get in the rearview.

During Month Fifty-Five I must have thought a hundred times, "Oh, I should write about THAT." Every time, I never did. Whatever on the reasons why: Days were crazy. Time is elusive. Moments move on.

But then we hit last Friday, May 31. The final day of a month that had already beaten me up ended up being the most crushing of them all: our family had to put down our beloved dog, Fisher.

It's not a good memory, or one easy to write about. In fact, it's one of the hardest I've ever lived through. A big statement when I've gone through hospice with both my mom and dad. But May 31 with Fisher—which was actually the anniversary of my dad's death—is now a double marker of our lives. Not to record it would be disrespectful to the greatest Wonderdog that ever lived.

Everybody loves their own dogs and thinks they're the best. I get that. But Fisher was one of those dogs that other people also thought was incredible. I wasn't even interested in having a dog when we got him, but Wes and I were engaged, and he conned me into going to the CMPD Animal Care and Control shelter one afternoon. Once you're at a shelter, with your fiancé begging you for a dog, there's not much chance you're going to leave empty-handed. There were a couple active, cute puppies in the playroom where you can hang out with rescues you might potentially take home. This little white-and-brown soft thing was the most quiet. The most shy. He kept curling up in my arms, didn't yelp, and just hung out. They told us he was about fifteen weeks old, found alongside a suburban road. It was assumed, the workers told us, he'd been thrown out a window because of some injuries he had. He was little and adorable with a chocolate patch of fur over one eye. I finally broke down.

Wes and I took him home that day and named him after the spot we would be getting married months later: Fort Fisher.

He trained himself. I swear to you, he literally taught himself to put his paw up on the door when he wanted to go out. He'd then leave and return to the door when he was done. As he got older, he learned to back up into bushes to do his business most of the time, with no clean-up needed. He rarely barked. He could chase tennis balls and walk on a beach forever without stopping until you wanted.

Fisher was always the only one up when I came home from work at midnight, or later. He'd wait on the couch. When the key turned, he'd pop his spotted head over the back of the sofa to catch my eye. By the time I stepped inside, he'd be in front of my feet, tail wagging.

But the best part about Fisher? By far?

He didn't need a leash.

This is a ridiculously fantastic fact. You could let him stay beside your hip or walk ahead or behind, and he'd obey traffic laws. He'd stop at streets to let cars cross. He'd move over on a sidewalk for other people to pass. He'd sometimes forge ahead to assure the path was safe for you to approach. We broke every leash law in this city. Why not? He did everything right. Some neighbors used to get mad, but most learned to love him strolling by, looking like he was alone. We'd hear some yelling, "Hey, Fish-Man!" as he trotted in front of their porch. He often seemed more human than dog; Fish-Man was a solid nickname.

There were moments, of course, I'd be stopped by someone who would sternly say, "YOUR DOG NEEDS A LEASH!"

I'd pull a leash from my bag and put it on. They'd walk away feeling like they'd done their civic duty.

I'd then let him drag a leash with no human attached.

To admit this now seems safe. No more Fisher to give me a citation over.

Parker always called Fisher her "older brother." In some ways, she was raised to think she was the second child. You can judge. That's just how it was. So much so that when Parker was born, her birth announcement was a black-and-white picture showing part of her head, but more of Fisher's snout kissing her weeks-old scalp. The headline read *Fisher's New Toy.* In smaller font was her name and weight.

I got *lots* of pushback on that one: how I could make my first human child's birth announcement more about a pet than the baby?

Because when you love your dog, and you bring home a seven-pound infant, having them love each other becomes a number-one requirement to you as a new mom. That's how.

Birth announcement aside, whatever was done to foster that relationship worked. Even when Hutch came, it was still Fisher and Parker as besties.

Last Friday morning when she said goodbye to him at the bus stop before she headed to school—and she knew he'd be gone when she got back—it almost broke me. She hugged him and told him she loved him forever. She was sad and strong. Amazingly strong. She'd had some time to think it through and knew it was for the best. Then she straightened up and asked me, "Mom, can I get a locket?"

I must have looked confused.

"So I can put a picture of Fisher in there and wear it around my neck?"

Oh, God. My words caught in my throat.

"Of course you can, baby."

I said it once aloud, but the same response kept cycling through my mind silently on repeat, drowning out every other thought in my brain as I watched her slowly walk up those bus steps, and turn around one final time to wave to him. The thought wouldn't stop. *Of course she can. Of course she can. Of course she can. She can do whatever she needs to do to learn and heal through losing the other half of your heart.*

I was waving like I always do, hoping to God the dirty bus windows blocked her from seeing the tears stream down my face.

CRLO

When you love someone—human or pet—you don't want to imagine them not being there. Even as they age, the thought of their absence is too big a hole, so you subconsciously choose not to focus on it. But three months ago, Fisher started hobbling on his right hind leg. We assumed it was arthritis. At thirteen years old, that would make sense. A biopsy, though, later determined it was bone cancer.

Pain medicine kept him going for a bit, but we knew Memorial Day weekend at Kure would be his final beach trip. Parker threw a tennis ball for him for an hour along the water's edge early one morning. I sat with my coffee watching them with wet eyes. He didn't want to let her down and tried hard to chase every toss. Despite the pain of osteosarcoma, he never gave up. They eventually walked back to me, her content with fingers lightly resting on the top back of his now-salty fur coat, him looking like he was smiling behind the tennis ball in his mouth.

The actual act on Friday was worse than expected. I'd never been through a process like that. Anyone who has knows exactly what I'm talking about, and maybe understands the difficulty in describing it. Fisher trotted into the veterinarian's office with a slight limp, but honestly seemed to be feeling better than he had in weeks. Wes and I kept looking at each other. Were we doing the right thing? We were taken into a room and the vet tech left the two of us with Fisher to have our "final time" together.

Even though we knew why we were there, the tech saying "final time" shot through both of us. She left, and both Wes and I got down on the ground with Fisher, who laid his head on my knees. It had always been one of his favorite positions. Wes started talking to him, lifting up his ear and rubbing behind his head. The longer Wes talked, the closer his mouth and face got to Fisher's fur. I'd never seen my husband such a wreck. He was telling Fisher how much we loved him and how he was the greatest Wonderdog in the world. Wes was so inconsolable it was the only thing that kept me half-together myself . . . one of us would need to be able to function enough to drive home.

Then the doctor came in the room. It was very peaceful. Fisher was staring at me, his head still on my knees. I looked in his eyes and slowly stroked his nose, and Wes kept his own face close to Fisher's as he rubbed his head the way they both loved. Suddenly, Fisher was no longer staring. His eyes were closed. We saw his stomach still. It was over. He was no longer in pain.

 glyph

Friday night was unnervingly quiet when I walked in after work. A dark, sleeping house. No greeting. No tail-wagging.

Getting Parker's locket was what our family did all day Saturday. We drove around Charlotte to find a small sterling heart necklace and print

out the best tiny two pictures from their last weekend at Kure together. That necklace is her newest prized possession. She wore it to sleep last night.

But—and I mean this—Fisher is absolutely better off. Wes and I are adults and can heal through the emptiness. Parker feels comforted by her locket. Hutch, thankfully, hasn't been impacted. And as my brother Warner said about Fisher's current state of happiness, "I bet there's a beautiful greenway with a leash law for him to break in Dog Heaven."

Run free, Fish-Man. We love you forever.

---

*COMMENTS:*

 **Molly.** Hutch and Fisher.

 **Molly.** A portrait of Fisher as a puppy hangs in a prime living room spot.

**Matt M.** I can only imagine that this is his view in heaven. You posted it once and I saved it because it reminded me of our family dog's love for the ocean.

**Amy Q.** Oh my. Tears are flowing.

**Terry G.** I used to think that people who loved their pets like you've expressed were nuts. That was before . . . before our son got Lady and she later became mine. She and I became soulmates. She taught me love like I had never known and made me a better person.

**Kim L.** Fish was a great dog and you gave him a great life. I knew you were going to be a great mom way back when you first got him. He would spend the night sometimes [at Noda Bark & Board] when you were working crazy hours. You would come pick him up first thing in the morning and take him across the street to the park. No matter how tired you were you would always throw the ball for him until both of you were exhausted. I would watch you and my heart was happy with all that love. No doubt Fish is running free and chasing tennis balls until he drops. Thank you for sharing him with us all these years. Much love to all you. P.S. I miss him under my desk already.

**Christy S.** This is absolutely beautiful. What a lucky boy to know such love from your family. And what a lucky family you are to have had his love and devotion. The locket is perfect.

**Dolly H.** My heart sank when I saw the post the other day with Fisher. I knew . . . "Land of the Free," you said. As if he was heading to run free. We just had to make that horrible decision two weeks ago for our 17-year-old Lucky Dogg. He was our baby just like Fisher was yours. We have followed posts about Fisher and always look for them. I'm sorry.

**Cathy B.** I have two dogs I love with all my heart and I know that day will come for me as well. Because of Parker, I will now buy a locket.

## Appendix

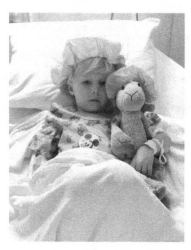

Hutch is "king" this weekend. He did so well with an out-of-nowhere emergency surgery on Friday—one week after we had to put Fisher down—we're rewarding him with being the head decision-maker. So far, he has ordered McDonald's with chocolate milk for lunch, owned the remote control, and declared Lambie as second-in-charge. Makes sense. Lambie went through surgery with him.

Jokes aside, Hutch is now absolutely fine. (Please re-read that part: *He is absolutely fine.*) But turns out "my belly hurts" meant his appendix was gangrenous—nasty and dead. It thankfully did NOT rupture, but was leaking yucky stuff into his body, and because he's only four and not able to describe actual pain, silly me assumed he was constipated.

The ONLY reason we made the pediatrician appointment Friday afternoon was that Saturday started two weeks of glorious Kure

Beach vacation. I just wanted to make sure—this sounds terrible now to admit—that he wouldn't be whining on the car trip.

Thankfully, the pediatrician took one look at him and sent him to the ER.

Good lesson: If your young child doesn't have a vocabulary large enough to accurately describe pain but tells you something hurts ... believe them. I'll never doubt again.

Lord knows, Hutch is happy today. The inside pain is gone, antibiotics are helping with everything else, and he only had to spend one night in the hospital. We are extremely grateful for the quick-actioned, kind surgeons, doctors, and nurses who made Hutch—and Lambie—feel incredibly special. Lambie had his own bracelet and Band-Aids, which helped immensely with Hutch's fears.

Removing an appendix is a common surgery, though not always for four-year-olds. But again, he's fine, and our family is just anxious to hear Kure's waves, a few days late. King Hutch says Lambie is also excited to learn to swim.

Life rolls on. When it rains, it pours.

---

*COMMENTS:*

**Keliah M.** The beach heals everything.

**Renee C.** Thankful he's feeling better. I'm sure a doughnut from Britts will cure completely.

**Carl P.** Don't worry you didn't believe him; just be happy you got it checked.

## Surfing Mermaid

"Mom? Do mermaids surf?"

"Sure. Why?"

"Because that's a girl out there. See her? Maybe when I grow up I can be a mermaid AND a surfer."

⊂◈⊃

Thank you to the many women who teach our daughters they can do anything they want . . . even when they have no idea of the lessons they're passing on by example.

*COMMENTS:*

**Susan H.** I am still hoping to be a mermaid.

 **Molly.** Me too. .

**Cynthia G.** We always told our children they could be anything they wanted to be. One night, at a family dinner, our beautiful 8-year-old super skinny daughter announced she had decided what she was going to be when she grew up: "Sumo wrestler!" she exclaimed with great pride. We fell completely silent . . . but no one told her she couldn't.

**Lisa M.** Thirty+ years ago my husband and I would go to Kure Beach and there was a female lifeguard. She would go out past the breakers to about where the young lady is in this picture. She would swim back and forth for what seemed like hours! I told my husband if I start to drown, send her after me. She was the strongest swimmer I've ever seen.

## Healed

Took a solid week after surgery, but this little nugget is feeling 100 percent back to himself.

## Mermaids for Life

Touching tails.

## MONTH FIFTY-SIX: Beach to Mountains

Today my mermaid left the water and entered the woods.

Two weeks, overnight. Her second year at camp. This year she was taller and older than at drop-off last year, but what struck me most was internal growth you can't easily see. Last year Parker was cool in her independence, but still hugged us hard when we said good-bye. This year she hardly had time to wave. She'd just linked arms with a new girl—I caught her first name, but not where she was from, her age, or anything else—and they ran off together. Fast friends.

It's a gift, isn't it? To be young and effortless with relationships.

Anyway, while Parker moves forward in summer break, it's back to work tomorrow for me.

In remembering this year's June vacation, the look-behind starts with wishing to forget. The glorious two weeks in June our family desperately looks forward to every year began with Hutch's emergency surgery, a week after Fisher had to be put down. Our run of bad luck continued in Kure with trips to urgent care for Parker, Hutch's longer-than-expected recovery and intense bathroom issues, five Walgreens visits in two days for antibiotics, three days of rain, and me backing my car into a pole, shattering my rear windshield. Kids are oddly perplexed when they see an adult mess up. P and H were in the backseat fighting and the second the cruuuuunccchhhh spppppppppllllllllllaaaaattt crrrraaaaacckkkk-kkkkkkk happened, they both got eerily quiet, with a sixth sense about the shattering glass being the straw that would be breaking Mama's back.

Annie's attitude about the sun and tomorrow are right, though. It does come out again. Eventually, medicines kick in. Eventually, windshields get fixed. And eventually, Kure ended up being an email-free mental break where time meant nothing.

Here's the digital scrapbook for this year:

- Surgery, urgent care, the windshield. (Get those out of the way.)
- Sleep. Enfolded me like ocean depth, almost every night. Sometimes I crashed by 8 p.m. One night, Parker even put me to bed.
- Britts for breakfast. Britts one day even for lunch.
- Family Monopoly.

- Hutch, four, learning math by paying rent on properties his sister owned.
- Mermaid tails.
- Visiting two sentimental boardwalk fish.
- Hutch calling spaghetti "angel noodles."
- Freddie's.
- Beach House Burgers.
- Morning walks with Yeti coffee.
- Jellyfish everywhere. Parker got lightly stung and didn't know it. (She thought scratches were from a seashell.)
- Her flips and dances and dives.
- Cartwheels across the width of the beach.
- That dang carnival. Will the Carolina Beach rides be there forever?
- The Pier. Being what the Pier always exactly is.
- Celtic Creamery. Four times.
- Lifeguards leaving at 5 p.m.
- Finding that artist! He wood works with hurricane debris; his talented wife paints what he carves. Their beachy shop in a storage unit is a gem.
- Golf cart travels. Wes was obsessed.
- Hutch's unsurprising obsession with the cart's keys.
- UNO Attack.
- Missing *The Little Mermaid* movie viewing at the lake.
- Proving to kids I used to swim competitively.
- Black-and-white pictures in blue-gray frames.

- That empty lot beside the cottage that's now a million-dollar duplex.
- The beach beautifully wider than ever. Guess that dredging/ re-nourishing worked.
- Parker demanding suntan lotion. (She learned!)
- No makeup. Not one stitch. Not one night.
- Gem mining.
- Book reading.
- Crab-leg cracking.
- Ferry riding.
- Ring diving.
- Feeling free.

Kure is my sanctuary from the world. Even sometimes from myself. It's where my thoughts seem more clear. Maybe your peace is found in the mountains, or inside a childhood home. Maybe it's on a sitting rock, or in a hammock, or bumping along a back road in a beater truck. I love all those things, too. But it's Kure that brings me peace. Crossing over Snows Cut Bridge onto Pleasure Island where Carolina Beach, Kure, and Fort Fisher sit, puts a level of bliss inside me that feels like air: weightless and shapeless and drifting.

Thank you, Kure. Once again, thank you.

Parker's breathing in the mountains tonight, but I'm preparing to head back to reality and the grind here in Charlotte.

I'll be ready.

*COMMENTS:*

**Carolyn D.** I do understand that feeling of the beach; in 2001 my husband passed away after years we had spent at Ocean Isle. I continued to go the OIB every year at the same time we visited for several years and it gave me so much comfort and peace. I'm glad you're home (I've missed you!) and glad the kids are healthy.

**Hillary E.** Your bullet points bring back many of my own family beach memories. Peace.

**Brenda M.** I loved your comment, "No makeup. Not one stitch. Not one night." That's me when I spend the month of September at my place in Garden City, SC. Relaxing, doing whatever I want.

**Pam W.** Love your writing! But I have to admit, I missed you on my TV.

**Ricky Y.** Even with everything you listed, good and bad, sounds awesome. Welcome back.

**Wayne R.** Nothing like the beach to set your mind at ease and your soul to realize what is important in life.

## Camp Moms

Graduated Chapel Hill together as great friends. Now we live in different states. Today, we met by coincidence.

"Ellie?"

"Molls?!?"

We could've predicted lots of things twenty years ago, Ellie, but not that decades later we'd meet again while picking up daughters who are the same age, bunking in neighboring cabins at the same summer camp.

# JULY

## Step Back in Time

Taking a special, once-in-a-lifetime gift of a trip to a remote, unique place in Michigan called Mackinac Island. I was born here. I have a bazillion early childhood photos, but no real memories of the place. When serendipity makes it possible to visit decades later, you go. Fancy dinners, no cars allowed, and horse-drawn carriages feels like a step back in time.

Which, actually, I guess it is.

More to come...

*COMMENTS:*

**Stephanie W.** That's where they filmed Somewhere in Time!

**Leon S.** My most favorite place in the United States.

**Melissa T.** I want to take all my friends there. I grew up in MI and have a million memories.

**Kathy J.** We are also from Michigan and love Mackinac Island and the Grand Hotel. Getting on the boat gets me so excited. Enjoy being back in your original home.

**Arlene S.** I spent my vacation there several years ago. Loved the scent of lilacs and the lunch at the Grand Hotel was unbelievable!

## MONTH FIFTY-SEVEN: Snapshot in Time

My dad. He's on the left, head turned, laughing at his friend. Late 1960s, Mackinac Island. His friend's name is John.

This week, fifty years after this photo, John and I met.

I'm an open book, but sometimes I worry . . . do I put too much put out there? But I've been at home for five days now, and last week's Michigan trip remains in my head. Some people talk to friends when they have lingering thoughts they need to process, while others sort through their feelings with time spent alone. My way of processing is to document and record.

Mackinac's significance to my family began decades ago. My baby photographs show me in bonnets, next to horses, and as a toddler held firmly in the arms of Grand Hotel employees. My dad worked there. He was a young manager who had somehow found his way to the resort from Smithfield. My mom was from Lancaster, Pennsylvania, and had found a summer job there working in its lobby retail shop.

A southern man and northern woman, both experts in hospitality.

They met. They dated. Then dated long-distance. Eventually, they married and lived in a townhome at the bottom of the Grand Hotel hill. They had me. After two years, they moved to Pinehurst. Soon after, they divorced. I was three and my brother was three months.

By the time I hit kindergarten, my mom had moved us two kids back with her to her hometown in Pennsylvania.

That's all I ever knew.

Clearer memories came in the years that followed. My dad remarried an amazing woman and I got two more remarkable brothers. My parents remained a wonderfully friendly divorced couple, shuttling my brother, Jay, and me back and forth between two states. Mackinac was a reference to a time and place in the past.

It's human nature as you get older to wonder more about each step of your journey, sometimes to pass down to your own kids, and sometimes to satiate your own curiosity about where you came from. So, recently, I've wondered more. But in my case, there's just no one to ask.

Life is a series of opportunities, though, and sometimes fates align in timely fashion. There was distant family on my mom's side—people on the island who knew my dad and loved my mom—who out of nowhere this summer, invited us to stay. "Bring your own kids, please," they said. "Come back to your first home here at the Grand."

We went. The four of us. It took two airplanes, a shuttle, a ferry, and a horse-drawn taxi carriage, and suddenly we were

staring at the mile-long Grand Hotel porch.

Parker asked if it was a princess castle. Hutch couldn't understand why the island did not have cars. And the pool. Oh, he loved the pool! He also loved the old-school silver keys that turned a lock to each resort room. No digital swiping key badge. He couldn't get over it.

For five days, we lived a trip where we did new things. Bike rides around a seven-mile island. Up 207-steps to an arched rock. Swimming in Lake Michigan fully dressed—my mermaid dove right in. Fudge. Much fudge. Dressing up for dinners. Teaching manners at the fancy restaurant. Sno-cones at the pool. American flags flapping. Walking back and forth down the long white porch. A painted chess board with human-sized pieces to move. Learning to ignore the smell of horse poop and living for the smell of geraniums.

We made lots of new memories.

And, as the black-and-white picture of my dad and John indicates, the emergence of some old-new ones.

CRUJO

While lunching with Mom's second cousin one afternoon, a man approached us.

"You're Joby Grantham's daughter?"

I instantly got up and hugged him. Didn't even think about it. He must have thought I was half-nuts to not even ask his name first or reach out a hand. But he hadn't said Joe. He hadn't said Mr. Grantham.

He'd said Joby. A nickname only known by long ago friends.

"I was his roommate in the late sixties," he said. "Your father was quite the bartender back then."

Bartender? My eyebrows must have risen.

"In a carousel bar." He laughed. "There were merry-go-round horses spinning behind us as we served drinks. He was charming. The ladies loved him."

I never knew dad had been a bartender.

John talked about visiting my dad in Smithfield, and stopping by his college dorm for a weekend in Tennessee, and how even after John was drafted and spent nearly three years at war, my dad welcomed him home. How once my parents were married, dad worked long hours at the Grand and my mom would call, sometimes hysterical, unsure as a new mom what to do with her crying baby. What to do with me. John said my dad would walk down the hill to comfort her. How one time my mom called and John beat my dad down the hill by taking a bike. He went to help his buddy solve the problem first.

I was laughing and glassy-eyed, gloriously grateful to hear these missing puzzle pieces about my parents' lives. After a while we hugged goodbye.

An hour later, sitting outside a cool butterfly conservatory on this small island we had taken the kids to as a tourist attraction, John came flying up on his bike.

"Here." He handed me an old 5x7. "I went home to find it."

I looked down and saw that photo at the top of this chapter.

"That was your father," he said, laughing. "Everyone's friend. You knew you liked him within the first eight seconds of meeting him. Thought I still had this around somewhere."

Seeing Dad there. A younger version of what's in my mind. Almost like I could touch him. I grabbed for my phone. "Can I take a picture of this picture, please?"

"Oh, it's yours." I looked up in disbelief. "I'll be gone at some point," he said. "And no one will care much about this photo once I'm gone. But I think maybe you'll care. I think maybe you'll care lots. That's why I went home to dig around. You should have it."

❧

John's right. I do care lots. A week later, I'm still thinking about him and the miraculous trip and beautiful lunch with my mom's family, and a magical carriage ride tour around the island, and the fact my dad was a bartender who charmed the ladies. I'm laughing at the thought of him standing on the hotel's porch, dressed to kill, when he was in his late twenties and early thirties. I really laugh thinking about John flying down a hill to help his buddy help his wife, who was a new mom, struggling with me as a crying newborn.

Last week we made new memories with the kids, but also relayed past stories from unlikely storytellers. I absolutely love this picture that two weeks ago I didn't know existed. I also love that tonight there's another more current-day snapshot of me standing next to the man who was standing next to my dad fifty years earlier.

You can caption it: John and Joby's daughter.

---

*COMMENTS:*

**Steven F.** Dapper as all get-out.

**Annie A.** A gift for anyone to learn things about their dad and mom that they did not know.

**Richard F.** Feel like I was right there witnessing all this.

# AUGUST

## Norman Rockwell

Just like Norman Rockwell, except a conference room instead of a kitchen. And Taco Bell instead of home-cooked. And asking her not to roller skate around my office instead of talking about our days. Yup. His exact vision.

---

*COMMENTS:*

**Warrior J.** A full-time working mom. I get it.

**Sylvia E.** And that, my friends, is family gettin' it done.

**Jeannette P.**  Totally. I saw Norman Rockwell right away.

**Debe M.**  #ModernParentingForTheWin

**Wendell R.** The roller skates kill me.

## He Still Fits

*COMMENTS:*

**Amie F.** Even though they don't "physically" fit for very long, they forever have that spot even when their legs and arms spill out all over the place.

**Philip M.** Nothing like a mother's love, to know you're safe.

**Edlana.** Security.

## MONTH FIFTY-EIGHT: Lawless Leash-ness

Laughing (and loving) this surprise award posthumously honoring Fisher as the "best and most stealth leash law violator."

Fisher had an incredible life. I still get mad cancer got him.

When missing him, I always go back to the fact he walked himself. You'd let him out and he'd come back. As I've admitted before, we weren't great followers of Mecklenburg County's leash law.

But that's why my friend Melissa's surprise plaque means the world to me. She's a dog person. A rescuer and an employee, actually, within CMPD's Animal Care & Control. She was there thirteen years ago when we adopted Fish-Man. She said after hearing we had to put him down, it took her a few months to come up with the right gift because she knew how special he was. When one of our news photographers went to interview her this week for a story on dogs . . . she asked him to bring it back to put on my chair.

You'll find it now forever placed on my desk.

We still miss you, Fisher. Be certain, there might be another dog joining us in our house sometime, but you will never be replaced.

## Still Waiting II

Once again, the start of school.

## Best Friend

First day of third grade, and Parker's teacher gives a get-to-know-you assignment: fill out a newspaper sheet with your personal "exclusive" story and a picture that explains your life best.

What matters to her most.

# SEPTEMBER

## MONTH FIFTY-NINE: Unlikely Friends

The sweetest life relationships are the ones you don't expect.

I've had an overarching thought this month about Hutch in social situations. The way he interacts with people is perplexing. I say this knowing that you never know who, what, or how your kids will turn out, and maybe twenty years from now I'll look back and think, *Oh! That was a sign of who you are now!* Or, maybe, today's thoughts will cause a massive chuckle, because by then, he will be the complete opposite of how he was as a child.

With that said, Hutch's interactions with other people have been a back burner thought for years. I am not *concerned*—that's way too strong a word—but there is an awareness about how he communicates with others. Wes and I have talked about it at length; he agrees that the way Hutch approaches a person or group is far different from his sister. She's easy. She makes friends, has friends, brings up other kids' names all the time, meets people with no thought or judgment, and jumps around socially with ease.

He does not.

I confidently assume the distinction between the two is normal. Girl versus boy. Older versus younger. Or just two different personalities within two different children. They work their little worlds in different ways.

Hutch zeroes in on specific individuals. Much like he does on specific things. He loves his preschool class, but talks constantly about just one boy and one girl. If we go to the park, he'll find one friend. If we put him in a new soccer or karate class, it's a build-up all week to get him ready for a new crowd. Once there, he'll be in the center of other kids, but won't care about the group around him. Instead, he'll attach himself to one or two others, and only if absolutely necessary. He happily enjoys small circles.

None of this is bad. Just notes a mom keeps in her head as she watches her children grow.

But with that as a background, maybe it makes more sense why Hutch's adoration in this picture for a neighborhood buddy is so special. The two of them are an unlikely friendship. There's an obvious age gap: Aidan is thirteen and Hutch is in preschool.

Aidan's family is wonderful. They are longtime friends who live down the street. We've watched Aidan grow into a mature eighth grader, and Aidan has watched Hutch go from baby to toddler to a little boy who's aware he's one of the youngest kids in our neighborhood. Aidan watches Hutch get understandably left out when older kids take off on bikes with more freedom and fewer rules. Aidan has always, with no exception, been good to Hutch. He includes him in touch football games, helps him with a sled during snowstorms, and always makes Hutch feel older when we're all together.

This adds up to Hutch thinking Aidan is his best friend.

CR&O

Weeks ago, in a beautiful twist of goodness, Hutch got to spend the night at Aidan's house. Hutch packed a bag with care. He took his blanket and Lambie and certain toys to show off. He followed Aidan around for twenty-four hours, went to his baseball game, and Aidan made my baby feel like he was on a legitimate best-buddy sleepover, instead of a last-minute childcare issue with Aidan's mom becoming our savior (endless thanks to you, Shelly).

This picture is just one of many from that evening. Aidan proved wrong every story you hear about teenagers being selfish. He jumped on a trampoline with Hutch, ate ice cream with him, talked about the Carolina Panthers, and played little-boy games for hours straight.

Look at how Hutch looks at Aidan, and how Aidan lets him.

Hutch's relationship with Aidan is also a flash of truth about how much kindness matters. From all ages. To all ages. After that over-night, I've seen Hutch do small things and say certain things he must have picked up from Aidan and thinks are cool. His big-boy, "best-friend" influence is everywhere.

Mentorship comes in all forms and sizes.

Here's to never forgetting the importance of child adoration.

---

*COMMENTS:*

**Joe A.** I can't love this enough. Awesome job, Shelly, on raising an exceptional young man. Aidan, you are going to change the world. Thanks Molly, for sharing this friendship. It is one that will last a lifetime. And the lessons learned will build onto an already impressive youth.

**Diane W.** Oh, how I love this story! Reminds me of my son and how he had the ability to help make smaller children feel important and included them in activities. He's now the father to four precious little boys and is a super-involved daddy, continuing to shower this sense of self-worth and love on these precious children.

**Jane W.** Thank you for sharing. Aidan, you must be an outstanding person and friend.

**Fallon C.** Molly, I completely understand . . . my son (only child) and his cousin (only child) are 8 years apart. My son has grown up looking up to his big cousin whom at one point told everyone that was his big brother. He was the little kid at all the baseball, basketball, and football games and adored by the big kids. My son, who's now 11, looks at his cousin who's now 19 and used to think his cousin's friends were his friends too, and they did just that. They played with him and loved him for him! I have many pictures of his big buddies coming to his games once he was old enough to play and watch him. It's a wonderful memory.

**Becky H.** It has been a beautiful thing to watch our children go from being the little kid in the picture to being the big kid. Good, loving community begets good, loving community.

## Gala Girls

"Mommy! We look like the tables and chairs!"

This crazy, intense, demanding, lovely, and magical job of mine puts me in positions to get in the community and overpack my schedule for events and give-backs that feel amazing inside. I know that most moms don't get the opportunity to go to black-tie affairs very often. But I do. And no shame in it. I'm proud to take part in these causes.

But tonight marks the first time I brought my funny and smart eight-year-old as my evening date. We went to the Ronald McDonald House Storybook Gala. Seeing the night through your child's eyes—especially a party that helps children not as healthy or as lucky as your own—is a gift in itself.

---

*COMMENTS:*

**Renita S.** We stay at the Ronald McDonald House of Durham & Wake frequently for our daughter's care at Duke. It's one of the biggest blessings in our lives.

**Lauren H.** I've loved taking my kids to this sort of thing since they were old enough to be mature by my side. Little kiddos are cute, but bigger kids are FUN!

**Patricia H.** "Tablecloths and chairs!" That's classic. How kids view the world.

# OCTOBER

## Not Today.

**From:** Grantham, Molly
**Sent:** Monday, October 07, 2019 6:32 PM
**Subject:** RE:

Thanks for this nice note. Really appreciate the kindness. It's always wonderful when women work hard to lift other women up.

-Molly

**From:** ████████████████
**Sent:** Monday, October 07, 2019 5:51 PM
**To:** Grantham, Molly <MGrantham@wbtv.com>
**Subject:**

Hello Molly,. Your hair looks terrible every day...Very striny & unkept. And please, don't even say you don't have time. No excuses.

---

*COMMENTS:*

 **Molly.** It's not always men with the harsh judgment. And as I said when the Twitter troll went after Parker, you don't always have to delete or be quiet. Replying when warranted feels great.

**Kathy G.** Perfect answer for a striny person.

**Amanda R.** I admit my first thought was, *"She should not blackout her email."* If someone is going to write it they should own it.

## Birthday Bacon

A big bacon birthday breakfast for my boy. Five years ago today, he was already eight days past his due date, content to go nowhere. Laid-back then, and even more so now. You bring unique joy to all those around you, Hutch. We love that you're too much. Happy day to you.

---

*COMMENTS:*

**Mandy M.** No way. Has it been five years already?

**Laura H.** Happy Birthday, Hutch. Killin' it with style today wearing that watch.

**Samantha S.** OMGosh, Seems like yesterday I saw a pic of him as a babe, eating sand at Kure.

## MONTH SIXTY: Calendar Worker

This kid. No one like him. Which I suppose every parent might feel justified in saying about their own child—you get to see everything they never show everyone else.

It's unreal for me to type "Month Sixty" and know that is the time passed in Hutch's life. You guys have been watching his little mind grow for years—you know about his work passes, watches, his obsessions with key chains, access codes, cars, trucks, and having his pockets/bookbag filled with any particular gear he's determined he needs before letting himself walk out the door.

Have I ever mentioned his natural draw toward company logos? Hutch is a marketing director's dream. You can barely drive with him because he points out every billboard. He can't read, but he knows them. "There's Jersey Mike's!" "There's a Ford car shop! "If you want to get Dunkin' Donuts, Mom, one is coming up!"

There are the logos on TV, too. He watches commercials and says the company before it's shown. He'll know by the music and sometimes even the font, that the ad is for Publix, or a brand of jeans, or a restaurant. He'll then say the tagline out loud before the tagline is said at the end by a big voice.

I don't know where it will eventually lead. But I do know right now, he's thirsty for knowledge . . . but only knowledge that fits the chess board in his mind. I study him, desperate to unlock clues. Every week I learn something new about what he's trying to teach me about how he works.

Which leads us to this picture. His morning ritual begins with crossing a day off his wall calendar. It is no-questions-asked the first thing he does when he wakes.

The wall calendar was a gift last year for Christmas. I mean, he likes order. He's definitely a systems guy. He likes knowing what days are "work days" and what days are "family days." Plus, at some point, he'll be in kindergarten and need to know days of week and months. So while I thought it might be a little beyond his age, I went for it. Made him his own calendar through Shutterfly, with personalized photos for each month.

Short of the ice cream truck, it has been one of the best gifts ever.

All year long this calendar has helped him make sense of our crazy family schedule. It creates structure and dictates days. The calendar is like . . . his brain on paper.

He knows every single birthday in our extended family—ones I can't even remember. He now also knows every birthday of every child in his preschool class, and every holiday date and what day of the week it actually falls on. Quiz him. On any date. You'll get a response like: "Christmas is December 25th and it is on a Wednesday."

Ask most children what they want to be when they grow up, and you'll get a couple standard answers. (Parker's currently are: an actress, a soccer player, or . . . ahem . . . a news reporter.)

A year ago, Hutch answered, "An ice cream server."

A few months ago it changed to, "I want to be a calendar worker."

Pause. Pause. "What does a calendar worker do, Hutch?"

"Works with calendars."

If you need a worker of calendars, I've got your five-year-old.

Sometimes he hums to himself about days, weeks, months, and years, or what weekend plans are three weekends from now. Last week, Hutch said with no prompting, "November 28th is Thanksgiving. This is the same month as Grandpa's birthday, which is November 10th on a Sunday."

It's a special way of processing. His pediatrician said she doesn't believe he's on the autism spectrum, and I've asked. Entering school next year will help figure out what it means about his learning style. Right now, his doctor just thinks he's a smart kid and we should enjoy his nuances and remarkably hysterical way of loving life.

Done.

It's easy to appreciate how he notices details other kids (and adults) don't usually see. You never know what will fall out of his mouth because his mouth is connected to a brain that works differently. It makes anyone around him laugh out loud every single day.

Both a challenge and a fantastically beautiful mind to raise.

---

*COMMENTS:*

**Patti B.** My grandson is a bit like Hutch, he loves order and lines up all his cars, toys, soldiers etc. This weekend when I had them and took he and his sister out for a play date, he said, "Mimi will you trust me to tell you how to get us home a different way?" At the stop light I secretly typed their address into the GPS, then said, "Sure son, let's go, you've always been terrific at directions." Lo and behold, he got us the 30-minutes from Charlotte to Monroe and didn't miss a beat. His mind works very differently, but he's smart as can be.

**Jennifer B.** I schedule things all day long. Sign me up for HCS . . . Hutch's Calendar Service. I'll be his first client.

**Tammi E.** Oh, the places he'll go.

**Savannah H.** (preschool teacher) Yes! There are times I can't even remember my own birthday, and he will remind me.

## Cotton Candy

I don't know her, but somebody get this woman a Volunteer of the Year Award. I asked her—she said her name is Ruth. She's at an elementary school festival. All in. Present. Assigned to this station and had never before worked with cotton candy, but is now an expert. She told me—while not looking at me, dedicated to the core as sugar flew around her mouth while half-sticking in her lipstick—that her grandson is in first grade at this school. She simply came to help support him and his school.

The face of grandmotherly love.

*COMMENTS:*

**Leah Z.** Nice to meet you today, Molly. Ruth also told me that her grandson couldn't even make it to the event. HE WASN'T EVEN THERE. Rock star volunteer.

**Joy M.** I used to work at a cotton candy factory and if it wasn't for the over-clothing and hair bonnets we had to wear, we would have looked like this. If you went outside, bees wouldn't quit buzzing around your hair.

**Amy M.** I can't stop laughing! You go, Ruth.

**Jessica K.** Ruth and all the other grandparents, parents, neighborhood volunteers, high school and college volunteers are the ones who make it bearable to come to work and teach day in and day out. They inspire us with their commitment. Even teachers need to see others "buy in" to give us a little extra motivation.

## Watching from Afar

Tuesday is dance night. I picked up Hutch and brought him with me to watch during my dinner break. He's a statue. He stands and stares through that glass as if he can't bear to miss one second of any move she makes. Because honestly, he can't. She is his entire world. The adoration of a younger sibling continues to be the most incredible thing I've ever witnessed.

*COMMENTS:*

**Sharon O.** Every night during her pregnancy my granddaughter would read to her stepmom's belly. On the day of delivery, that baby waited until her big sister arrived at the hospital and spoke to the belly. She told her, I am here now, come on out. Eight minutes later she made her appearance. This was the look they gave each other shortly after her birth.

**Amy S.** AMEN. I am so glad you have instilled this in your children. We had our son and daughter 2 years apart. As soon as we came home from the hospital, my son wanted "his sissy" to "play in his room." From that moment on, I would put her in her bouncy seat so she could watch him. I'm convinced this is why she walked at 8-months so she could keep up. I worried this would change once school entered the picture, or different schools, but they only grew closer and closer. Both going to WCU, both staying in better contact now that that oldest has graduated than they do with us, ol' Mom and Dad. At every stage, it just gets better and better.

**Mary B.** This is what happens when you leave for college! Ripped my heart.

**Phil R.** Maybe HE wants to dance too! My grandson loved it, for a couple of years until baseball became more fun.

**Corey P.** Wonder if he would want to join her?

## Braids

Parker took a screen grab of a hairstyle she liked for her Halloween costume tonight. This morning she woke me extra early with a brush.

"You've got to do it before school, Mom," she said. "You'll be here on break to trick-or-treat, but you won't be here to get me ready."

Her voice held no anger, sadness, or blame. Only a tone that showed she was trying to figure out how to make it work. Children adapt. It's okay if you miss some moments, because children adapt.

I'll say that again: It's okay if you miss some moments, because children adapt.

*COMMENTS:*

**Cheri M.** She solved the problem on how to make her hair happen. This is a win.

**Brittany N.** Yes they do! I've been crazy busy lately and we had an overnight trip planned for tonight. This morning I realized I'd forgotten to make plans for someone to let our dog out. I texted my neighbor only to find out that my 11-year-old had already made arrangements with her. Not only do they adapt, but they will also take initiative when you least expect it.

**Melissa K.** I couldn't do that hairstyle at 3pm in the afternoon after I'm wide awake, so kudos for you for getting it done first thing in the morning.

**Mark K.** She has fantastic time management skills.

# NOVEMBER

## Text From A Preschool Teacher

> Can you or Wes please start checking Hutch's lunch before he leaves home, his lunch today consisted of a Dr Coke and a cheese stick.

How I just learned wickedly conniving son has been secretly taking out what was packed in his lunchbox and replacing it with what he wants from the refrigerator before we leave the house. Just when you think you have things under control and are becoming a model Mom with systems in place and kids who follow rules, your wrist gets slapped and you're forced to check yourself.

---

*COMMENTS:*

**Joyce L.** At least he wasn't sneaking old clothes of his older brother and changing into them when he got to school. My daughter had the school thinking we were destitute.

**Karen J.** Molly, it could be worse! A coworker's (teacher) son packed his lunch and couldn't find an ice pack. So, he grabbed the next best thing. A frozen cocktail pouch!

## MONTH SIXTY-ONE: "Just Make Sure It's Playful"

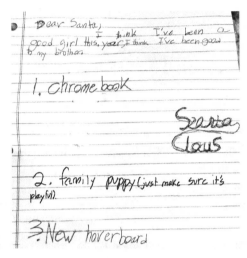

In our house, Santa brings three things. We've had that rule forever. It was advice from friends soon after Parker's birth. The thought behind it was that if you make children choose three things, it teaches priorities and (maybe more importantly) doesn't break your own bank every year.

Parker has taken months to prioritize. The #2 you see here is not whimsical. She knows I've said no to a new dog for now . . . but she also really wants one and misses her best friend.

I know I've said we'd get a new dog and do believe our family will get one at some point. But Parker is all about specifics, and every time she asks me when, my gut flip-flops on the answer and I've been careful to never land on a concrete timeline. She'd hold me to any actual date. And candidly, it's nice not to have the responsibility of a pet right now. I know Parker wants one, but at eight years old, a dog wouldn't fully be her responsibility. It would be me and Wes as caretakers. Late-night walks when I come home from work, vet appointments, heartworm pills, training . . . every time I think about a new puppy, I think about what it takes to turn a cute puppy into a family dog.

Then I think about Fisher and the huge addition and love he brought to our lives, and how happy he made us all.

How happy, especially, he made Parker.

Then today she hands me her list. After listening to me waffle on answers and never give her a day and make no real promises about bringing another dog into the home, she took it upon herself to try and get one here the only way she knew how. Now I'm staring at this list, stuck.

My logic knows we're not ready . . . but Santa makes dreams come true, right?

---

*COMMENTS:*

**Jennifer E.** I'll see your puppy and raise you a desperately wanted guinea pig. (Nope.)

**Biscoff G.** I love how she specifically points out that she's been good to her brother.

**Lauren M.** My mom told us growing up that Santa had a rule: he doesn't bring anything alive that eats and poops.

**Cristin G.** We told our kids that Santa is not allowed to transport live animals.

# DECEMBER

## Road Trip Car Forts

"Here are two blankets. Each of you build a fort where you can't see the other and see who can be the quietest."

---

*COMMENTS:*

**Julie S.** Another fave of mine is "the statue game." Who can pose and stay still the longest?

**Caryn A.** We play the bubble game. This means each person has to hold air in their mouth/cheeks, whoever holds it the longest wins. Makes for a nice long quiet ride.

**Tracy S.** When my children were little, we'd tell them we were driving through a quiet town and anyone making noise would be arrested.

**Jennifer B.** And the winners are . . . Wes and Molly.

## Stacy Hunsucker

Everything just clicked. This beautiful young wife. Her death. Why this headline today has been bugging the back of my brain so much.

All day we've been reporting about Stacy Hunsucker, a young mother who died of a poison commonly found in eye drops that can cause heart stoppages. Yesterday her husband was arrested. Prosecutors say Joshua Hunsucker, a paramedic, gave his wife doses of that poison. Today he was charged with first-degree murder.

It's a stunning headline. Stacy was young, happy, and they had two little girls.

And it just hit . . .

. . . She was also Hutch's preschool teacher.

All day I've been reporting blurbs about this story, and never realized I was talking about "Miss Stacy" until just now.

Hutch loved Miss Stacy. We all did. She had a heart of gold.

She died last year a few weeks into his three-year-old class. The preschool principal called one night while I was at work.

"We think it was something to do with her heart," she said, her voice choked with emotion. "None of us really know. Her husband said they were watching TV together and then she just fell onto his shoulder."

It didn't make sense, but . . . lots of headlines don't make sense. None of her coworkers at the church school were going to question the oddity. Parents of the kids she taught certainly had no reason to wonder. Sadly, hearts just sometimes stop. Maybe there was undiagnosed heart condition nobody knew about, even in someone so young. I remember the preschool principal saying Stacy was in her early thirties and did have a pre-existing medical situation.

At the time of her death over a year ago, Stacy's cause of death was listed as "natural."

Then today it came out in court that it might be something much more sinister.

Every single person is innocent until proven guilty. Including her husband. I'm writing this at a time when we don't know what evidence will come out in court, or why prosecutors feel they have such a strong case against him that they can bring charges. Time will tell.

For my purposes in this moment, it's just a sickening feeling to put it all together that the poor woman who is dead at the center of today's movie-plot-like news is the same smiling, sweet mom of two girls who loved my son as if he was her own.

Headlines that are personal always hit harder.

*COMMENTS:*

**Whitney K.** So sad, very scary that her husband, a paramedic, did this to her. Praying for her family during this difficult time.

 **Molly.** To be fair, I'll say again, innocent until proven guilty. He's charged, not convicted. But it is a stunning headline.

**Shannon G.** Stacy was one of a kind! I got the privilege to work side-by-side with her in a preschool classroom together. She was the best co-worker ever.

**Jami C.** It was a devastating time in our world when she was gone. We've been best friends with Stacy since we were young. She was as beautiful on the inside as she was on the outside. She didn't deserve this, but we will get justice for her sweet soul and those precious girls.

## Rudy

Merry Christmas from our whole family, including the newest member brought this morning from Santa. His name is Rudy—but today we'll call him Rudolph.

## MONTH SIXTY-TWO: Matching Pajamas

Time off at home with zero plans is underrated. If you've never tried a staycation, give yourself the gift. It's glorious. For the past ten days our family did no holiday traveling, had no goals, woke up with no schedule, and wore no fancy clothes. Instead we ran around outside, cleaned two closets, cooked at home, made too many cookies, ate junk food in restaurants, played 5,943 games of UNO Attack*, and enjoyed a new puppy.

Rudy's getting acclimated. As this picture might indicate.

Our eleven-month-old Labrador-mix-with-terrier?-bully?-unsure? needs more explanation.

He came from Santa, but Parker first met him weeks ago at, predictably, CMPD's Animal Care and Control. If we were going to get a dog, we'd go there, if for no other reason than to honor Fisher. I still couldn't decide if Santa would actually deliver but took Parker to the shelter anyway.

You know, just to look.

"You need to get some idea of what type of puppy or dog you want," I over-explained. "You want to give Santa more instructions."

She methodically walked up and down the aisles in between the kennels. Big dogs, small dogs, super hairy hundred-pound dogs, beautiful Huskies with piercing blue eyes, a gray bounding forty-pounder I loved, sleepy dogs, yippy dogs . . . she walked by them all. She stared intently at their faces and broke the rules by sticking her hand in to love on any whose nose got close enough to touch. She repeatedly questioned how they'd all find homes. She laughed at a cute li'l guy who couldn't stop chasing his own tail. She was walking and looking and walking and looking, and suddenly stopped at kennel #12-C. Inside was this blond mutt lying on his stomach, head tucked down and curled into his legs.

Unlike the others, he was quiet.

"What's his name?" She asked my friend Melissa, who'd sent the sweet plaque about Fisher for my desk weeks ago. She was walking with us.

Melissa read the tag. "Looks like his name is Rudy."

"Hey, Rudy. Hey Buddy." Parker suddenly sounded like a toddler. "Can we get him out so I can play with him?"

Melissa, of course, obliged. Moments later, I was watching Rudy nuzzle up to Parker in that exact same cinder-block shelter playroom where Wes and I had first met Fisher thirteen years earlier. Parker and Rudy formed a connection. I saw it happen in front of me. My head was swimming with memories of cuddling a fifteen-week-old Fisher as I watched my daughter—only a figment of my imagination back then—talk to this huge puppy as if they were both human. She stared at him, mouth laughing and open, her heart coming through her words.

"I think he likes me, Mom!"

P fell in love that afternoon. It was hard for her to leave Rudy, but she did, knowing she now had specifics—as in the exact dog—to send Santa.

Every single day after that shelter visit, Parker mentioned Rudy somehow, in some manner. Not begging. Not whining. More like he was just top of her mind. I told her how tons of dogs need homes and usually, a dog finds you. If Rudy was meant to be for her, Santa might make it happen. But if he was meant to be with another family, he'd make that family happy. I made no promises. Even then I wasn't sure I was ready, and I knew Wes wasn't. He said he'd go along with it if I felt it was best for Parker, but made it clear he didn't think our family was emotionally prepared for another dog. I understood what he meant. Despite her pleas and Santa request, Fisher is irreplaceable. That hole still feels big in moments.

At eight years old, Parker accepted the "if it's meant to be, it'll be" with more maturity than I thought possible. She didn't pepper back with constant follow-ups, just seemed curious as to whether Rudy would find his way to her.

In the meantime, I couldn't stop remembering the way she'd talked to Rudy in that small shelter room. I broke down. I called Melissa, and together we concocted a plan. She put him "on hold" for me. I told Wes what I'd done, and knowing he'd already said he'd go along with whatever decision, he nodded silent acceptance of our pending new family member.

Days before Christmas on a morning before I went to work when Parker and Hutch were in school, Wes and I went and secretly got an XL crate that could collapse flat, along with a leash and dog food. We stored everything in the back of his car underneath office supplies the kids never get curious about. On Christmas Eve at 10 p.m., after the kids were asleep, Wes drove to the shelter and picked up this sixty-pound baby we knew very little about. How would he react to us? Our home? Freedom?

Wes trotted Rudy into our home before midnight. Rudy—amazingly—didn't bark once. After Wes and I took turns rubbing his tummy for an hour and creating Christmas under the tree with the other items on their short lists, Wes took him to a guest bedroom where he had set up the crate. Both of them slept there.

I fell asleep in our bed, knowing we were now locked in, and anxious to see how Parker would react when she saw Santa delivered not just a puppy, but *the exact puppy*.

On Christmas morning, the kids came running into my room. They were so excited about rushing downstairs, they didn't even question Wes's absence. I quickly texted him in the other bedroom and told him we'd be down in two minutes. He texted back he'd be ready.

Two minutes later, I let them rush down the steps together.

Rudy was there. He was sniffing around the tree with a blue collar and a leash attached, trailing behind.

Parker's reaction was almost indescribable. Pictures capture it well. They show the distinct difference between pure joy and just excitement. Hutch was excited. Period. A new dog! But what you could see in Parker's eyes was something deeper.

"It's MAGIC, Mom!" She said on repeat. "Santa brought him here. Santa got him out of the shelter with magic. He brought him HERE. OH, RUDY! You were meant to be with us!"

I said this with stories about Mutt and will say it again: it's special to believe in something bigger than yourself.

ভ৩৮৩

The last five days have been a stark reminder of what having a puppy does to sleep schedules and shoes you leave lying around. But Parker is learning, trying to take him out, walking him often, and he's almost already house-broken (??!?). It only took him two nights to sleep in a dog bed and not roam around the house peeing. And our vet says he passed his checkup with flying colors.

The biggest issue is his strength. When he sees another dog walking, he about takes our shoulders out because of his intense leg muscles and desire to either go play or show dominance . . . I'm not sure which. Guess we'll work on that.

Overall: Rudy has been a huge success. Most of all, we all love him.

Anyone who has ever rescued a dog knows: shelter animals are grateful. We don't know where Rudy came from or how he was treated before now, but we know he's gentle enough with kids and wants to get so close to us sometimes, it's as if he's trying to crawl inside our bodies. He clearly never wants to go back to whatever it is he came from. He knows his past and lets us know he likes the present better.

Merry Christmas to Parker, yes. But as she said to me Christmas night, an even bigger present to him.

"We got a new dog, Mom," she said. "But Rudy got his forever home."

Exactly.

CR∞

*For the record, when I say 5,943 games of UNO Attack . . . I mean Hutch has won more than half of them, fair and square.

*COMMENTS:*

 **Molly.** Don't mock me. Rudy's name is embroidered on his pajamas. How mortifying that somewhere along the way I became that person.

**Connie De.** My Brooks, also a lab mix came from ACC, taught us unconditional, goofy love for eight years before crossing the rainbow bridge. My heart is still broken. I rescued Leo, who fills my heart, but the void remains.

**Joyce H.** Rescues are the best.

**Lee D.** Molly, I get it. We rescued Charlie from near death in Kuwait thru KARE Kuwait. One-(yes ONE)-month-old with cuts and a traumatic head injury (all man-made) but he is here now and 8-months-old and loves his new home as much as we love him, and wouldn't have it any other way.

**Stacy J.** It's amazing how dogs find you.

# JANUARY

## Sunday Love

Things seem to be going well.

---

*COMMENTS:*

**Lane P.** There was a connection at the shelter. She will have love with Rudy that will be in her heart forever.

**John N.** You saved another life and you will get unconditional love fur ever.

**Gloria N.** Santa will always be her hero.

## Rudy Report

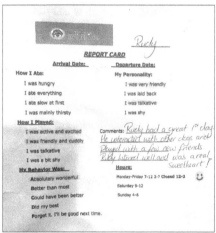

After spending two weeks running around like the crazy eleven-month-old, sixty-pound baby he is . . . jumping with muddy paws on everything . . . today, Santa's four-legged gift went to get out some energy. Bless the doggie daycare NODA Bark and Board for this first-day report card. He's invited back. I've never been this excited over actual school reports for either of my children.

---

*COMMENTS:*

**Robin H.** Wait until he is so excited to go he talks on the way there. My brother's husky starts howling when dropped off at doggie daycare.

**Luann B.** I do believe Mamma is starting to love the 4-legged present as much as her baby girl.

## I Lose

Home-from-work 1-a.m. greeting.
    Rudy: 1
    My favorite heels: 0

## A Personal Announcement

Our New Year Surprise. Exciting and insanely scary.
   We just sold all the baby stuff this summer.
   You never know what twists and turns life will throw.
   Give me a minute to breathe.

*COMMENTS:*

**Leann M.** Oh my goodness! I'm so excited! And not just for another baby . . . but that there will be a lot more adventures to write about.

**Michelle M.** I noticed the other day when I was watching you on the news you had a different look about you.

**Maggie L.** Such a stinkin' cute picture of both of them. I am so excited for you and your family all the way from Chicago!

**Dana F.** New dog, new baby. I see second and third editions of a book.

**Belva B.** I prescribe a maternity leave at the beach the whole summer.

**Dennis W.** Part III to your sweet and wonderful journal. A puppy and a baby. Be still and take in the moment. Congratulations.

**Debbie G.** Is that really a sonogram? Oh my God . . .

## Hutch Tooth

After asking once a week for almost two years about losing teeth . . . the first one fell tonight. Couldn't be prouder.

---

*COMMENTS:*

**Leigh F.** How much do those visits cost in this modern-day world?

 **Molly.** Leigh, our Fairy is still stuck in her own childhood and leaves four quarters.

**Mary B.** So glad you are having another little one for us to follow.

**Lisa D.** Few years ago while teaching preschool, one of our students was really eager to lose his first tooth. While on the playground he finally lost it and I mean LOST it and we never did find it. He could have cared less, just so thrilled to show off that snaggletooth grin.

## Ikea Room

High time Parker gets a big-girl room in her same amount of small space. Went to Ikea. Brought home seventeen boxes, so figuring about fifty-six hours ahead.

## Loft Bed, Desk, and a Dresser

Fifteen boxes in. End in sight after eight million hours this weekend. Taking a break for Super Bowl and grateful for any reason to do anything else.

When we opened all the boxes at once, Parker said, "Oh, Mom! It's like doing a real-life Lego."

## MONTH SIXTY-THREE: Tic-Tac

I've had time to breathe.

Tic-Tac is the baby's name, at least for the next few months. It's non-gender-specific, implies tiny, and Hutch likes saying it. He comes in my room every morning and puts his face to my stomach and pajamas—talking so closely my skin feels his breath through the material. He says goodbye when I leave for work in the same fashion. Before talking to me, he has a full belly-button conversation with Baby #3.

It has been announced. The kids are beyond excited. I'm on TV every night showing, and at times afterward fielding ignorant emails about why I'm "getting fat," or, and these are nicer notes, whether I'm "expecting?"

All those things are facts. But being pregnant with a surprise child when you're over forty, into life with a demanding career and two active children already, is more than facts. It's feelings. And fears. Mentally, I've had a hilly climb the past few months. There is no reason not to admit my head-space struggle. Life was GOOD. Life was SET. Hutch starts kindergarten in August and we were DONE. Tunnel light was right ahead, yet I'm now due with a new baby . . . In JULY? Inches from the goal line of both kids in full-time school?

Having young kids and a big job with a 2 p.m.-to-midnight schedule has been a true joy the past almost-nine years (I can't believe Parker will be nine soon), but also, hard. You guys know some of the frustrations. Facebook, your comments, and the ability to "talk" to a moving world outside while sometimes feeling trapped inside a house, has been a gift.

Despite these tough moments, I've done it. Nothing is perfect and I continue to make plenty of mistakes, but I'm nine years into the juggle and proud of my children AND my job. There are plenty of past moments when I missed some after-school event, or when the rat race felt extra heavy, and in those moments . . . always . . . I always thought . . . wait. Wait just a bit longer. When they're both in school, it'll be easier. That's the message the world whispers to parents. Isn't it?

*Keep going: Once your mornings are fully free, you'll catch a little breathing room.*

Which is why—right or wrong—August of this year has loomed as a coveted mile marker in my life. Which is also why—right or wrong—when I first found out I was pregnant, a clear image came to mind: standing at the bus stop this August, waving them off, with a four-week-old in my arms.

The image made me want to cry.

The thought of starting over felt deeply scary.

⊙₰

I'm no longer in that spot. But years from now, when Tic-Tac owns my heart the same way his/her brother and sister do, it'd be good to remember the real conversations I had with myself these past couple months. Here's the unvarnished chronological truth from these self-talks:

1st: I'M WHAT??!!?

2nd: NO. No, no, no. THIS ISN'T HAPPENING.

3rd: Actually, it is. Look down, Molly. There's jelly on your belly, the ultrasound shows something moving, and you can hear the fast-paced heartbeat loudly through that microphone-wand thing.

4th: That sound . . . I remember. A heartbeat.

5th: Gripping anxiety. I'm in the conductor's seat on a train for an unplanned trip.

6th: Or, am I even in the conductor seat? Or the passenger?

7th: You can do this. MOLLY. Yes, Me. Me talking to me. Get a grip. You are logical. You adapt well. You are a fixer. People come to you for help. You can figure this out. Right?? . . . (Wait . . . Can I?

CAN I?) . . . Yes. I can. Breathe. Breathe, breathe, breathe. Planned or not, you better start tracking this route.

8th: Damn straight I can do this. I can do anything.

9th: On board. Let's research. Google "pregnant over 40."

10th: ForTheLoveof, IHateGoogle. Don't ever Google "pregnant over 40," then click any link with the word risks.

11th: Calm. Breathe.

12th: Go back to look at the video of Parker and Hutch's reactions. That's all there is to know. (You can see the video at http://tinyurl.com/3rdannouncement.)

Really, that IS all there is to know. Parker and Hutch's excitement grounded my fears, and Hutch kissing Tic-Tac twice a day is about as sweet as it gets. Now that we're at Week Sixteen with this pregnancy, I'm more calm. It just was, and still is in some moments, a mental tectonic-plate shift. But at least now I can say though I don't know how everything will fall into place with a newborn in our lives, I feel confident it will. It will be awesome.

While being a little crazy.

Here's another realization to confess. People—mostly women, but some men—are stopping me in grocery stores or writing personal emails about their own lives and thoughts. Those of you doing this are saying honest things. Things that acknowledge the fact I didn't start having children until later in life, while sharing your own similar stories. It's a stark reminder of how being over thirty-five, or forty, and having kids is very, very common.

These conversations with strangers are making me think heavily about our current-day world. Our society as a whole is teaching girls to go after their own dreams and be who they want to be. In many cases, that means focusing on education and career-climbing. It doesn't mean every woman chooses professional development, or has to, but it does mean more options are out there than decades ago. That's a good thing.

Meantime, national research also shows a massive jump in the age women are starting to have kids. As of 2018, the overall age to have a baby in the US was over 26.5, according to data from the National Center for Health Statistics. In 1980, the age was 22.5.

Daily anecdotes are further proof: more women in their late thirties and forties are dropping kids off at preschool. In the business world, you also hear about more companies adding childcare to keep and recruit female employees. On a micro level, every single one of my interns in their early twenties—all wickedly quick-witted women with huge potential and big future hopes—ask about how to manage kids AND a career? Not one of them, at least at their age, can see a future that doesn't include working.

Fact is, more and more women want both. Conversations with you guys are helping me gratefully see how the optics of a female, solo-anchoring a main newscast in a big city, a woman who is now pregnant and past the typical age to be so, sends an instant message that life can be on various timetables. None of us need to do things the same way. Figuring it out on your own is a good lesson to learn.

It's comforting to think Tic-Tac and his home in my growing

stomach might be helping show this without ever having to say a word.

Which leads to my new vision for August.

Here is what I now see:

I'm still standing at a bus stop, with Tic-Tac asleep in my arms. Or maybe a stroller that I'll soon dig through a dusty shed to pull out and clean. Parker and Hutch are excited, but before hopping on the bus, they both kiss Tic-Tac's head to say goodbye.

I'm no longer crying.

---

*COMMENTS:*

**Jennifer R.** All I know is that I'm incredibly grateful for your brutal honesty, the fact that you want it all, and that you are, most of all . . . open. I feel like I'm one you your "Molly's Kids" whenever I get a chance to glance at one of your posts. I'm also a mom of three. Most days I miss. I feel like I fail. I'm trying to survive, and my husband of 17 years passed from glioblastoma, after a 32-day diagnosis. Hardly time to even spell it. That was two years ago. I've learned to adapt . . . to be strong, to figure out this life, but thank you for making life so real. For loving all the things that make you, you. And for making wanting it all okay. I have a family, I have a career, I have a social life, and I have a story. I can say all those things with pride. I am inspired by your story, your heart for every source that fills it, and the smile that it leaves on my face rather it's through laughter or tears.

 **Molly.** You are powerful. Your words are extremely powerful. If you ever feel doubt, go back and read this comment and what you wrote about your own self and what you're accomplishing.

**Darlene H.** I only wish your sweet daddy was here to see them all.

 **Molly.** Me too, Darlene. Me too.

**Timothy H.** As a single parent I can appreciate your honesty. It is the hardest job on the planet. I admire the fact that you put this post here for the world to see that being a parent is not all unicorns and lucky charms. Thank you for showing what many of us have hid or are currently hiding. A privilege to see it in writing.

**Callie D.** All surprises come with a reaction, but few will share the good and the scary. I can't wait to see you in August, rocking yourself down the street with two kids ready for school, and Tic-Tac in your arms. So many females want a career and a family. Thank you for showing how career and parenthood can integrate (I do not believe in "balance") beautifully.

**Sallie W.** I was nine when my mom had her surprise pregnancy (At age 40 after moving to Africa and delivering at a tiny, rural Zambian hospital). My little sister was my real life "baby doll" and I still feel a little like her mom at times.

**Jennifer G.** Molly, thank you for giving hope to those of us who still want children . . . but are in our late 30s.

**Guenn CLT Radio.** Truth telling. Love you for it. Congratulations of course, children are such miracles. But I feel you. Whew. I'm in Countdown mode to them all being in school too and the thought of starting over, man. That's tough.

**Wanda R.** Who cares if you are over forty? Age is just a number.

**Madeleine M.** Keep on juggling.

# FEBRUARY

## MONTH SIXTY-FOUR: DNA Does Not Dictate

Reminder this weekend inside UNC's Student Store: DNA does not dictate personality.

I told P and H they could each pick one treat from the candy aisle. We were there on a day trip to visit my alma mater and to appreciate the beauty that is Chapel Hill. Parker immediately went over, scanned the rows, picked Twizzlers, returned them to me, and never thought about it again. Thirty seconds. Bam. Done. No regrets.

Just like how I do things.

This photo is Hutch.

Tormented. Too many choices. Overwhelmed. Likes too many things. Doesn't want to have to pick just one. Can't, actually, pick just one. Too hard to choose. "What if I get the wrong one?" He keeps pestering us all with questions. Lies down on his back to stare at the options from a different view. Holds multiple bags gingerly to study them closely. Twenty minutes in, he boils it down to two and asks everyone else around him which one they'd want. We all say the same thing: the octopus-shaped sour jelly gummies. He grips them, slowly walking to checkout. His demeanor looks like he's walking to a punishment. Head down. Dejected. In line for one full minute, he breaks out and rushes back to the candy section to look at all the options again. He starts counting the octopi in the bag he's holding versus how many plain gummy bears were in the runner-up candy choice. Upon realizing there's more gummy bears than octopi, he thinks the entire decision is wrong.

"I don't knoooooooooowwwwwwwwwww."

The wail is painful. He's not being bratty. His head just hurts from the difficult decision. He drops. I snap this picture while trying not to laugh.

But it also had been almost thirty minutes, and I was done. I told him if he couldn't decide by the time I counted to ten, he got nothing. I counted. He couldn't even lift his eyes to look up, so weighted down from the heaviness of this decision. We left the store with him getting nothing and a big tear running down his face.

Fifteen steps outside away from the store he screamed, "I want the octopus! I'll take the octopus! I've decided!"

I held his little hand and went back in with just him. He picked the bag and, this time, walked to the checkout with conviction and a smile.

Siblings aren't necessarily similar. A reminder once again that all children are different. Just because you raise them doesn't mean you always understand them.

---

*COMMENTS:*

**Laura E.** I can so relate! My youngest is exactly like Hutch. Bless her. We've learned to give her very specific parameters for souvenir shopping on family trips.

**Frank D.** Our middle child does the same thing. We get in line, all of us choose first. When it's time to pay, we tell her to choose so it doesn't take as long. Her siblings know this. She knows this. She hasn't changed. She's 24.

**Megan M.** My youngest daughter is like Parker. Decisions made in an instant. My oldest is like Hutch, struggling to decide which is the best choice. It's amazing how different siblings can be.

**Bee R.** He's such a detailed and thoughtful boy. I think with his personality, he may be considered a "highly sensitive." Not a bad thing; actually a great trait. Look into it, children can be HSPs as well as adults. I recently found out that I am. It explains why these situations are hard.

**Dede C.** My youngest is like this. After many times of me leaving a place with her getting nothing she was happy to tell me there was a name for her condition. She came to me and said, "It's called paradox of choice Mommy, I can't help it." I looked it up and never left a store without getting something for her again. Kids 5,343, Mom 0. They get me every time.

## Painted Shoes

This sneaky nugget was quiet for a good thirty minutes this past weekend. Wasn't until hours later I realized why:

He'd gotten into my craft basket, found paints, and was "redoing" his shoes. To each their own. Look at that proud artist face.

---

*COMMENTS:*

**Patricia C.** I worked as an artist for over 50 years and still paint as I'm addicted to it. I give him an A+.

**Brett L.** Kid's got skillz.

**Josefina C.** Painted the shoes to match his outfit.

## Rudy Sees Kure

Rudy's first last-minute trip to Kure. Joy was evident.

Think the dog had fun, too.

An exhausting thirty-six hours.

---

*COMMENTS:*

**Jan B.** Your girl has sand in her soul.

**Dee-Dee K.** Parker has really grown up.

**Krislyn C.** Last minute trips there are the best.

# MARCH

## MONTH SIXTY-FIVE: "It's a _____!"

You hope for healthy. Ten fingers, ten toes, good heart, everything intact and a nice long cry when they're born. Isn't that every
parent's roughly stated goal?

But there's no denying the mystery surrounding any woman's
pregnancy on whether she's carrying a boy or girl, and there was
definitely no denying that the suspense on that question in our
household had grown. Parker and Hutch were deeply obsessed
over Tic-Tac's gender—Parker wanting a girl, Hutch a boy.

The kids were making me batty every day, asking when they
could find out: brother or sister? And Hutch had taken to waking
me up—an unwanted human alarm clock—by poking me in the
face then trying to pull down the covers to kiss Tic-Tac through

my belly button to ask if he was a boy.

If finding out the gender would stop this morning insanity, I was on board.

Shelly—Aidan's mom—and I dreamed up a small plan.

She came by on Sunday night with her family, a cake, and cupcakes. Doctors and technicians had carefully not revealed anything to us during my appointments and ultrasounds, but we'd given Shelly access to look in the medical files. She laughingly said later, "Please double-check . . . it was listed as either XX or XY and I had to google to remember those old life science lessons on which was which!"

I still haven't double-checked as I write this, because she's the most thorough and responsible of friends and would never mess that up, but her confession rings true. Can you remember which set of letters means "girl" and which means "boy"? I couldn't. I still can't. It seems like such an old-school formal way of recording medical facts in today's modern world.

But I digress.

Back to Sunday night's festivities.

The kids had cupcakes filled with the icing that would match the gender of what Shelly had found. On "3 . . . 2 . . . 1 . . . Go!" we let them peel off the paper and dig in before we'd cut the cake she'd brought for all of us to share. It, too, had something special inside: either pink or blue M&M's.

The fast moments it took for Parker to rip down the brown wrapping around the chocolate muffin felt like a long time. She started biting, calmly yelling (she can do both at once), "I want to see. I want to see." Faster and faster with her thumbs and mouth simultaneously, half seconds ticking by like minutes.

Finally, she saw its color inside and shouted: "I know!"

Her face wasn't giving anything away.

Then we looked at Hutch. All of us.

The poor thing still couldn't get one bit of that cupcake paper off the muffin. He was no closer to knowing the gender of the baby than he had been seven seconds earlier.

"Oh, Hutchie . . . ," I soothed, worried he was feeling inadequate. "Do you see the icing? What do you think? Do you see it?"

He said nothing. Parker piped up. "He hasn't even wrapped his paper off."

I gave her an evil eye. She smirked in response.

"Hutchie! Can you see it?" I felt anxious for him.

He was painstakingly, little pull by little pull, peeling off the paper.

We all kept staring.

"Can I yell it out?" Parker looked at me again, the reveal on the tip of her tongue.

"No."

I turned to my five-year-old son.

"Hutch, do you see it?"

He took a mouse nibble, soft chocolate crumbs falling around his mouth and mumbled, "I don't see it."

"Take another bite, Hutch. Take a BIG bite this time."

He tried again. "I don't even see the frosting." Matter-of-fact. Not upset. My God, does this child move at his own pace.

"You got to go fast, Hutch," I said. "You've got to dig in."

"MOM . . ." Parker's impatient wail spoke for all of us in that room, mentally willing him to move faster. Though I remember thinking in the moment that I wasn't sure whether she was upset over not being able to yell the answer herself or the fact she didn't like the color she'd seen.

I walked over behind Hutch. "Come on, Buddy. Keep going. Get in there. Go the whole way in."

Hutch started eating off the top.

"HUTCH. Honey. You have to get into the center," I said. "Dig right in the middle."

We waited and watched and watched and waited and finally Hutch saw a bit of something other than brown chocolate in front of his eyes. He saw it at the same time I did, only he yelled instantly, not realizing how much thunder he was stealing from his older sister . . .

"IT's a BOY!"

Blue icing. Another baby boy.

Parker will remain the only hippie princess and Hutch will, finally, have someone looking up to him.

*COMMENTS:*

**Laura L.** What's crazy is how I read this whole story. Painstakingly slow, careful not to scroll too much and always sure to keep the next lines hidden so I wouldn't glance and spoil the surprise. Ha-ha! Congratulations!

**Carolyn D.** Seeing how patient you are with Hutch I'm guessing he takes after you; so I'm assuming Little Miss Hippie Princess takes after Wes?

 **Molly.** She is me. In every direction. I have never ever ever ever ever ever ever ever ever been called "patient" in my life. Until Hutch. He gives me no choice.

**Tiffany V.** We just found out we are expecting a boy as well. Our first child, due in August!

**Kristy N.** I was as impatient as Parker reading this, pulling for Hutch to take a big bite!

**Kim H-P.** Exciting! Little boys always love their Mama . . . no matter their age. Here's mine:

**Elisa D.** Congratulations Molly, Wes, and family! I love that you didn't do some sort of crazy "gender reveal" on YouTube, instead just writing it out. Just like you do. Just like we've learned to read and see it in our own minds. Wishing you all the best with the rest of your pregnancy

**Billie F.** Okay. I admit when I almost, almost got to the end I skipped ahead to see . . . I just couldn't wait.

**Katie O'S.** What a gift that you have these moments documented. I guess now we need to wait for the stories with #3 . . .

To be continued . . .

# AFTERWORD

I have an odd request. Here at the end of the book, I ask you flip back to the beginning and reread the dedication. It might have seemed haphazard when you read it the first time.

> *There is no goddess of surprise, but there should be.*
> *None of us know what's next.*

I originally had that thought—and jotted it down—while sitting at the hospice house years ago with my mom. When I decided to put this book together and found those words in my old notes, it seemed an appropriate place to start, remembering how uncertain that time felt.

Mom's death was swift and unexpected. My brother Jay and I didn't know what hit us.

Here I am many months later, once again being knocked down by surprise. This time instead of a surprise death, it's a surprise life.

None of us know what's next.

None of us know what's next.

None of us know what's next.

Which leads to where our world is as I write this. We're stiffled by a surprise pandemic. Nearly every country in the world is being impacted by a respiratory illness that has no vaccine or preventative antiviral drugs. Everyday life started changing for Americans a few weeks ago. Weeks before that, I had been reporting about the coronavirus on the news as a far-off headline in China; I remember reading stories here and there, and being curious enough to do some basic web searches to find out why it was so devastating in the Far East. But it wasn't in the US yet, so there weren't tons of stories published in the States.

Americans have great apathy for things until they face them directly.

A mere month after reading those news blips live on TV, the coronavirus is rampant. I'd argue every one of us is being hit in some form. Schools are closed, executive orders are in place for people to stay at home, and no group bigger than ten people can meet. The newsroom has been a ghost town. Our bosses sent most everyone home to work remotely. Since my pregnancy means I am considered high-risk, I was told not to come into the newsroom before 8 p.m. So I anchor the 11 p.m. show from the studio—where we now have 5 people at night (as opposed to the 15+ before)—and the afternoon/early evening shows are no longer my responsibility. This is the plan for the foreseeable future. I've been told to prepare for WBTV's technology team and chief photographer to come build a makeshift home studio in my house. It is probably needed sooner rather than later, but even the brightest scientific geniuses in the world can't guess a total timeline of when the coronavirus might peak, or, hopefully, fade.

Working from home half the day is what's best for Tic-Tac. I get it. Part of me wants to be in the newsroom more than ever covering this unprecedented event, and part of me wants to wrap myself in bubble wrap and drown in hand sanitizer. Wes and I are both working at home now, both of us trying to homeschool Parker through what's left of third grade and entertain Hutch all day because his daycare is closed. We are just two of the millions of parents in America adjusting to new schedules . . . and new balls to juggle.

The coronavirus could not have been predicted. An illness starting in one small village traveling through the world, killing hundreds of thousands of people along the way is a concept you'd think would be a plot for a novel. Not real life. Only, it is real. As real as real gets. People around us are dying, and we're all forced to live in these unexpected, difficult, altered times unsure of what's next. It made me question whether I should continue with publishing this book in this uncertain moment. Is now really the right time?

Yes.

That's where I landed after much thought.

Now is the exact right time.

Ultimately, the coronavirus will pass. A vaccine will be found and social distancing will stop being mandated. Life will move on for all of us, including my kids. Tic-Tac will arrive and Parker and

Hutch will continue to grow. The almost three years you just read about are already lived. Recording them won't change the future.

But the more important reason I believe it's okay to put this book out now is about an overwhelming sense of togetherness. This pandemic—that we wish wasn't happening—is, surprisingly (there's that word again), bringing people together. We are being quarantined in our own homes and looking out for each other by trying to keep apart. The coronavirus isn't just affecting one race, or age group, or geographical region. Everyone is going through some version of the same thing. It's no mistake the hashtag trending nationally every day reads: #AloneTogether.

That is how you guys make me feel when I write about real life and raising kids. Your comments indicate you sometimes agree with something I did, and other times wholly disagree. Either way, there's comfort in reading your words. You provide a relatability between our lives. Maybe in some small way, reading the stories and comments in this book can act as a reminder: we all have similarities, as we juggle different details.

As for what's next?

I don't know.

None of us do.

We can only hope we'll just add whatever might be thrown our way to the balls already up in the air, and keep managing them the best we can.

—Molly

# ABOUT THE AUTHOR

Molly Grantham is an Emmy-award-winning anchor and journalist in Charlotte, North Carolina. Besides her public and often nutty job, she balances motherhood, social media madness, and the swirling cycle of life. She graduated from University of North Carolina at Chapel Hill. This is her second book.

Molly continues to write monthly posts on her Facebook page: www.facebook.com/WBTVMollyGrantham. You can find more on her first book, *Small Victories*, and *The Juggle is Real* at www.mollygrantham.com.

CPSIA information can be obtained
at www.ICGtesting.com
Printed in the USA
BVHW071736040322
630613BV00001B/1